P9-DLZ-377

Jane Austen

WHO
WROTE
THAT?

WHO WROTE THAT?

Jane Austen

Heather Lehr Wagner

Foreword by
Kyle Zimmer

Chelsea House Publishers
Philadelphia

CHELSEA HOUSE PUBLISHERS

VP, New Product Development Sally Cheney
Director of Production Kim Shinners
Creative Manager Takeshi Takahashi
Manufacturing Manager Diann Grasse

Staff for JANE AUSTEN

Associate Editor Benjamin Kim
Picture Researcher Pat Holl
Production Editor Megan Emery
Series Designer Keith Trego
Layout 21st Century Publishing and Communications, Inc.

http://www.chelseahouse.com

First Printing

1 3 5 7 9 8 6 4 2

Library of Congress Cataloging-in-Publication Data

Wagner, Heather Lehr.
  Jane Austen / by Heather Lehr Wagner.
      p. cm. -- (Who wrote that?)
Includes index.
Summary: Describes the life and novels of the nineteenth century British author, Jane Austen,
known for her vivid portrayals of ordinary people in such novels as "Pride and Prejudice",
"Emma," and "Sense and Sensibility."
  ISBN 0-7910-7623-7
  1. Austen, Jane, 1775-1817--Juvenile literature. 2. Novelists, English--19th century--
Biography--Juvenile literature. [1. Austen, Jane, 1775-1817. 2. Authors, English. 3. Women--
Biography.] I. Title. II. Series.
  PR4036.W24 2003
  823'.7--dc22

JB
AUSTEN, J.
c.1

2003014409

Table of Contents

FOREWORD BY
KYLE ZIMMER
PRESIDENT, FIRST BOOK

HUMANITY IS POWERED by stories. From our earliest days as thinking beings, we employed every available tool to tell each other stories. We danced, drew pictures on the walls of our caves, spoke, and sang. All of this extraordinary effort was designed to entertain, recount the news of the day, explain natural occurrences—and then gradually to build religious and cultural traditions and establish the common bonds and continuity that eventually formed civilizations. Stories are the most powerful force in the universe; they are the primary element that has distinguished our evolutionary path.

Our love of the story has not diminished with time. Enormous segments of societies are devoted to the art of storytelling. Book sales in the United States alone topped $26 billion last year; movie studios spend fortunes to create and promote stories; and the news industry is more pervasive in its presence than ever before.

There is no mystery to our fascination. Great stories are magic. They can introduce us to new cultures, or remind us of the nobility and failures of our own, inspire us to greatness or scare us to death, but above all, stories provide human insight on a level that is unavailable through any other source. In fact, stories connect each of us to the rest of humanity not just in our own time, but also throughout history.

This special magic of books is the greatest treasure that we can hand down from generation to generation. In fact, that spark in a child that comes from books became the motivation for the creation of my organization, First Book, a national literacy program with a simple mission: to provide new books to the most disadvantaged children. At present, First Book has been at work in hundreds of communities for over a decade. Every year children in need receive millions of books through our organization and millions more are provided through dedicated literacy institutions across the United States and around the world. In addition, groups of people dedicate themselves tirelessly to working with children to share reading and stories in every imaginable setting from schools to the streets. Of course, this Herculean effort serves many important goals. Literacy translates to productivity and employability in life and many other valid and even essential elements. But at the heart of this movement are people who love stories, love to read and want desperately to ensure that no one misses the wonderful possibilities that reading provides.

When thinking about the importance of books, there is an overwhelming urge to cite the literary devotion of great minds. Some have written of the magnitude of the importance of literature. Amy Lowell, an American poet, captured the concept with her statement when she said, "Books are more than books. They are the life, the very heart and core of ages past, the reason why men lived and worked and died, the essence and quintessence of their lives." Others have spoken of their personal obsession with books, as in Thomas Jefferson's simple statement: "I live for books." But more compelling, perhaps, is the almost instinctive excitement in children for books and stories.

Throughout my years at First Book, I have heard truly extraordinary stories about the power of books in the lives of children. In one case, a homeless child, who had been bounced from one location to another, later resurfaced—and the only possession that he had fought to keep was the book he was given as part of a First Book distribution months earlier. More recently, I met a child who, upon receiving the book he wanted, flashed a big smile and said, "This is my big chance!" These snapshots reveal the true power of books and stories to give hope and change lives.

As these children grow up and continue to develop their love of reading, they will owe a profound debt to those volunteers who reached out to them—a debt that they may repay by reaching out to spark the next generation of readers. But there is a greater debt owed by all of us—a debt to the storytellers, the authors, who have bound us together, inspired our leaders, fueled our civilizations, and helped us put our children to sleep with their heads full of images and ideas.

WHO WROTE THAT? is a series of books dedicated to introducing us to a few of these incredible individuals. While we have almost always honored stories, we have not uniformly honored storytellers. In fact, some of the most important authors have toiled in complete obscurity throughout their lives or have been openly persecuted for the uncomfortable truths that they have laid before us. When confronted with the magnitude of their written work or perhaps the daily grind of our own, we can forget that writers are people. They struggle through the same daily indignities and dental appointments, and they experience the intense joy and bottomless despair that many of us do. Yet somehow they rise above it all to deliver a powerful thread that connects us all. It is a rare honor to have the opportunity that these books provide to share the lives of these extraordinary people. Enjoy.

A scene from the 1940 film version of Jane Austen's Pride and Prejudice starring Greer Garson and Laurence Olivier. The popularity of Austen's stories, which have been adapted for film and television numerous times, are a testament to how much they resonate with audiences even today.

1

A New Novel by a Lady

She had an excellent heart; her disposition was affectionate, and her feelings were strong: but she knew how to govern them.
—Sense and Sensibility

ON OCTOBER 31,1811, an advertisement appeared in England's *Morning Chronicle* newspaper. It described the publication of "A New Novel by a Lady" titled *Sense and Sensibility*. The author was credited only with the mysterious line "by a Lady" and her novel was soon being described as "Extraordinary."

Sense and Sensibility, the first novel by this unknown author, began with a very modest printing of less than 1,000 copies, packaged (as was common in that day) in a three-volume set that sold for about fifteen shillings. It carried the description "An Interesting Novel," which signified to nineteenth century readers that it was a love story. The publisher, Egerton's of Whitehall, had acquired the manuscript "on commission"—meaning that the author was expected to pay for the initial printing and to pay any additional expenses should the number of copies sold not equal the cost of publication.

The author was a woman with little money of her own, but she had confidence in her book. Soon it was apparent that she was right to be so confident. The book quickly received positive reviews which praised her characters, the believability of the plot, and the pleasing ending. The publisher sold out all of the copies, and the author gained a much-needed profit of 140 pounds. It was the first money she had ever earned herself, and it gave the thirty-six-year-old author a sudden sense of freedom.

Apart from a few close friends and family, no one knew that the author of *Sense and Sensibility* was Jane Austen. Austen had wanted to remain anonymous, fearing that she might be talked about, pointed at, or criticized. It was important for women of Jane Austen's day to exhibit ladylike behavior, and a lady never called attention to herself. In fact, Austen herself had once written, "A woman especially, if she have the misfortune of knowing anything, should conceal it as well as she can."

So Jane Austen worked quietly and secretly, writing the stories that were beloved by her family and then enjoyed by a much wider circle. Her identity would eventually become known and her writing would receive favorable attention, but few could imagine that her portraits of family life would one day place her with the greatest writers of English literature.

Sense and Sensibility was really the revised version of a manuscript Jane Austen had written much earlier, which she had completed much of in 1795. The earlier version of the story was called *Elinor and Marianne* and told the story of two sisters with very different personalities—an older sister who was sensible, and a younger sister who preferred to live life with feeling.

The story was told in the form of letters between the two sisters. However, the format made it difficult to develop the plot, as the two sisters needed to be separated when important events occurred in order for them to describe what was happening to each other. Austen put the manuscript aside for a while and then, in November 1797, she attempted a new version. Her new approach required her to completely rewrite much of the story, changing the format from letters back and forth between two sisters to a third-person narrative. She continued work on the novel through the spring of 1798, changing the title to the one with which modern readers are familiar: *Sense and Sensibility*.

It is impressive to think of a writer dedicated enough to completely rewrite a novel and change it in such drastic ways with such a stunning result. Yet it is even more impressive to learn that for the nine months before she revised *Sense and Sensibility* she had begun work on a draft of a novel titled *First Impressions*, and that after *Sense and Sensibility* was completed, she began work on the first draft of a novel called *Susan*. These manuscripts that served as bookends to *Sense and Sensibility* would also be revised and retitled—the first would be known as *Pride and Prejudice*, and the second would be known as

Northanger Abbey. In four years, Jane Austen created the framework of three major novels, and she was not yet twenty-four years old. But despite her impressive talent, true success did not come in her lifetime. She was thirty-six years old before *Sense and Sensibility* was published, and in between the time of its first draft and its final publication, she had known great difficulty and disappointment.

When the news of the publication of *Sense and Sensibility* reached Austen, she was living in a country cottage in the small Hampshire village of Chawton. Only about sixty families lived in Chawton, but for Austen it represented a wonderful change from her previous surroundings. Austen, along with her older sister and widowed mother, had spent several months in a variety of rented rooms in the large city of Bath and then traveled from one family member to another before a wealthy brother offered to provide the women with this quiet home.

It was 1809 when Austen finally settled in the cottage where she would write three new novels and find some small success. Before then, her life had reflected limitations; the family had little money, and she—as a single woman in her thirties—was thought to be past her prime. She had not married, and had no family money to make her somehow more attractive as a marriage prospect. Women of her class did not work, and so any small success and financial reward her novels brought was particularly sweet.

There was no lavish celebration when the news of *Sense and Sensibility*'s publication arrived. Her sister was away from home, and so Austen and her mother toasted the publication by taking turns reading out loud to each other from the printed volumes. Even this offered Austen little happiness; her mother paused at the

Jane Austen's home, Chawton Cottage, is now a museum. It is where she did most of her writing while living with her sister and mother along with a staff of three servants. It was the first time Austen and her family had found a permanent residence, and Austen settled into a disciplined writing routine.

wrong spots and did not properly read the dialogue. Instead of parties, Austen had to content herself with the fact that she could now buy a few presents for friends and family and that she could continue to write, knowing that others beyond her family might appreciate what she was doing.

Still, Austen continued trying to keep her accomplishment a secret. She wrote on small slips of paper, so that her writing could be quickly put away or covered up if someone came into the room while she was working. Between the front door and the room where she wrote was a swinging door that creaked. Austen refused to allow anyone to fix the door, because the creaking noise warned her that someone was coming and gave her time to hide away her writing.

Austen loved her home, and admirers of Jane Austen's writing can visit Chawton Cottage to get a glimpse of what her life was like. The house was located at the point where three roads came together. This sense of business outside her door was critical to Austen. She welcomed the opportunity to observe life but required a safe retreat from the world when she needed it. When the Austens moved in, the house was already 100 years old. It was shaped like an "L" and stood two stories high, with red brick walls and a tile roof. The front door opened directly into the dining room, and the ground floor also contained two sitting rooms: one with a piano on which Austen played every morning and the other where she did most of her writing on a small writing table.

Thanks to Austen's brother's generosity, the home was run by three servants: a cook, a housemaid, and a butler. Today, one would think a household with three servants indicated a substantial income, but in that time it was quite common for middle-class families to have several servants to help with the considerable labor involved in managing a house.

Part of the secret of Austen's success as a writer was her discipline. She had little privacy, sharing a bedroom with her sister and a house with three women. However, she woke up first in the mornings, going downstairs and playing the piano before anyone else was up. Austen was responsible for preparing breakfast, but it was usually a simple meal—perhaps tea and toast prepared on the fire in the dining room.

Then she settled down to her writing. She wrote from breakfast until dinner, the main meal of the day, which was eaten in the middle of the afternoon. Then there would be socializing with her family and any guests, followed by tea and then reading out loud to each other in the evenings. The family would read novels and Austen would often use the time to test her stories on family members. They were a sympathetic audience and helped her refine the dialogue and descriptions that characterize her novels.

Austen's life was a relatively closed one, marked by simple routines and interaction with family members and friends. She knew no other writers, and even after she became famous her circle of friends did not change in any substantial way. She remained at Chawton Cottage, reexamining and revising old manuscripts and writing new ones, sharpening passages and producing six wonderful novels that give a detailed glimpse of life in Jane Austen's day.

Austen left no diaries to reveal her inner thoughts or hopes. Her older sister, Cassandra, went through Austen's surviving letters and destroyed many of those that she felt portrayed Austen or the family in uncomplimentary ways.

Austen's greatest legacy remains her writing, and even in this she is careful to cover her traces. Her stories are not autobiographical, though they do reflect certain glimpses of their creator. Her novels focus on smart, serious women with strong beliefs and a desire to improve themselves. Yet there is a sense of humor that crops up throughout her writing, both in the situations in which characters find themselves and in the words and phrases they use.

Her novels provide a sense of what life was like in the early part of the nineteenth century. It was a life carefully observed—a world where manners and marriage mattered. It is amazing to realize that this woman, whose stories would be studied in classrooms by future generations, who some suggest transformed the novel as a form of writing, received little attention during her lifetime. Her name would become known, but she would never be "famous," nor enjoy any substantial financial success. She would outlive the publication of her first novel by only six years. While her writing is now well known, its author is not, and yet it is important to understand Jane Austen to appreciate her fiction.

Did you know...

In Jane Austen's day, there were few ways for women to be independent or to earn money. One of the only occupations open to women of her class—working as a governess, or live-in teacher—was not considered very respectable and did not pay well. The only way women of Jane Austen's class could get money was to marry or inherit it (only possible if a woman had no brothers). Jane Austen never earned enough to make herself financially independent. Her family's expenses were more than four times her earnings from her published novels.

From a quiet and almost anonymous life came books that serve as colorful, detailed portraits of life in the early nineteenth century. To fully appreciate the lives Jane Austen vividly describes in her fiction, one must first understand the life of the woman who created them.

Jane Austen was born in the Old Manor House in the village of Steventon in 1775. She was the seventh child in the Austen family, and at fourteen weeks was sent to live with a foster family until she was about two years old.

2

An Early Education

THE WINTER OF 1775 was marked by harsh weather in southern England. Snow and ice made travel difficult, and by three in the afternoon darkness had fallen. The news was equally harsh; the American colonies were in revolt, and British soldiers were being sent across the Atlantic to attempt to restore order.

In the small village of Steventon, about fifty miles from London, the rector's wife was expecting her seventh child. The rector, George Austen, served as the clergyman for the isolated village. He and his wife, Cassandra, had expected the baby to be born in November, but as that month passed they joked about their inability—after six other children—to accurately predict when the seventh would arrive.

The harsh weather kept the family's young children indoors, and their rectory home was crowded and noisy as November gave way to December. The rectory was located near the main road into the village of Steventon, but the road was narrow and winding and, in those days, muddy, unpaved, and full of ruts. The rectory itself was equally rough. It had been built in the late seventeenth century and then repaired before the Austens moved in in the 1760s. An extension had been added to the rear of the house, forming two wings.

A visitor to the rectory would find the clergyman's home full of the noise of active children. The ground floor contained three rooms at the front of the house: the good parlor, or sitting room, where guests were entertained; the common parlor, serving as a kind of family room; and the kitchen. Mr. Austen had a small study in the back, with a view of the garden behind the house. Upstairs, there were seven bedrooms.

The home, with its numerous bedrooms, exposed beams, and porch with a trellis, may sound large and rustic to modern readers, but to guests in the mid-eighteenth century it was seen as inelegant and unimpressive. In those days, the exposed beams were not a charming country touch but instead a sign of poverty. Members of the Austen family would, in later years, remember that the house had no cornices in the places where the walls touched the ceiling, then considered a sign of inadequate construction.

There were few villagers to help support the rector and his church. The tiny, gray thirteenth-century church of St. Nicholas stood apart from the village high on a hill. No more than 30 families lived in Steventon. There was no shop in the village and no inn for travelers. The rector was forced to become a farmer and a teacher as well as a clergyman to help support his family. George Austen tutored students in the rectory and raised cows, sheep and chickens. Cassandra Austen was always busy, not merely with her children, but in baking bread, brewing beer, and making butter and cheese. Despite their hard work, the family was frequently in debt.

On the evening of December 16, 1775, the baby that had been expected a month earlier was finally born. It was the Austen's second daughter, and they named her Jane.

The cold weather kept Cassandra and her newest child indoors for several months. On the sunny morning of April 5, Jane was wrapped up in a shawl and the family walked up the path to their father's church where the baby was christened. This was a public ceremony; because the risk of infant mortality was so high, she had actually been baptized at home by her father when she was one day old.

When she was about 14 weeks old, baby Jane was sent away from home to live with a foster family in the village. This must have been a traumatic event to the infant, to be separated from her mother and everything familiar at such a young age, but this was a system for raising her children that Mrs. Austen had followed before. The concept of bonding between mother and child was not a familiar idea in the eighteenth century; Mrs. Austen was not trying to be cruel in sending away her babies. She simply believed that the best way to raise them was to keep them with her until they were about three months old, then send them away to a local woman until they were about two years old—old enough to be more easily cared for at home. At the time, it was believed that infants, until they began to walk and talk, did not have real understanding or feelings, and that separation from home would not affect them. Jane's foster mother would have been paid to care for her, feed her, and help her as she took her first steps and learned her first words.

To reduce the chaos in the rectory, and to cope with difficult finances, one or the other of the Austen children was frequently sent away from home to live with friends, relatives, or foster families, or to attend school. Jane's brother George, who had been born ten years before her, spent most of his life in foster care. He had never developed normally nor gained the ability to speak (although Jane, as an adult, would mention speaking with him using sign language). Although he occasionally visited the rectory, he would not live there permanently.

When Jane finally returned home, she found herself surrounded by boys. Mr. Austen's tutoring had developed into running a small school for boys in the rectory. From February to June, and again from late August to late December, the house was full of students—some the sons of local, wealthy gentlemen, while others had traveled from a distance to live with the family and sleep in the three attics at the top of the house. The students—including the four Austen boys—were taught Latin, Greek, science, and geography.

It was not a large school as Mr. Austen took in only a few students at a time, and the cooking and cleaning were managed by Mrs. Austen more as if she had simply added a few more to her large family. The students played with Jane and her older sister, Cassandra. Mrs. Austen frequently entertained her children and the students with her funny, clever poems.

When Jane was nearly three years old, another baby arrived—a son named Charles. Just one week later, the oldest son, James, was sent away to school. He went to Oxford, which his father had also attended, where the fourteen-year-old vowed that he was going to become a poet.

The second Austen son, Edward, also left home in 1779. A wealthy cousin of the family, Thomas Knight, was newly married and on his honeymoon he visited the Austen family at Steventon. He and his new bride found the twelve-year-old Edward to be adorable and charming, and they asked for permission to take Edward with him on the rest of their travels. Edward went with them for the rest of their honeymoon, and the Knights became so attached to him that they frequently invited him to their home in Kent. Edward visited them frequently; they ultimately adopted him and made him the heir to their fortune.

Despite these two absences, the rectory was still full of children. For Jane, growing up surrounded by boys meant

Did you know...

Jane Austen's father served as the rector of Steventon Church. The rectory where the Austen family lived is gone, but the church still stands today, nearly identical to the way it was when Austen worshipped there. It is a simple Norman-style structure, thought to have been originally built around 1200. Austen was baptized in the church; her grandmother, oldest brother James, and his two wives, as well as Austen's nephew and other relatives and friends, were buried there. Memorial tablets mark the places where they are buried, and a bronze plaque inside is dedicated to Jane Austen.

that she became skilled at boys' games, and the children spent many summer days rolling down a green slope behind the rectory and horseback riding. The rectory had a large barn where the children played when the weather kept them from running around outside.

Growing up in a boys school also meant that Jane was exposed to learning at an early age. Her father had an impressive library, and the family spent a great deal of time reading out loud to each other. The children were allowed to read whatever they chose, and as soon as they were able they also began to write, creating word games, funny verses like their mother did, and skits to act out.

Jane was closest to her sister Cassandra, who was two years older. Jane and Cassandra shared a room. When Jane was six and a half, Cassandra went to visit her aunt and uncle, the Coopers, in the town of Bath. Cassandra's father went to bring her home and was surprised to find Jane and her three-year-old brother, Charles, walking along the road a long distance from home. They had grown tired of waiting for Cassandra to come back and had decided to go and meet her.

The Austen boys were taught at home until they were at least twelve, learning together with the other students. At the age of nine, Cassandra was sent away to a boarding school in Oxford, a school run by the sister of her Cooper relatives. It was soon decided that Jane too would go away to school. While boarding schools for girls were not unusual, it was not common to send away a seven-year-old to them. Mrs. Austen would later defend her decision, claiming that it had been entirely Jane's choice because she wanted to do whatever Cassandra was doing: "If Cassandra's head had been going to be cut off, Jane would have hers cut off too," she said.

When she was only seven, Austen was sent to a boarding school run by Ann Cawley in Oxford. When Mrs. Cawley moved her entire school to the port of Southampton, the town experienced an epidemic of typhoid fever. Despite this, Mrs. Cawley did not move the school, and Jane Cooper had to write her mother to let her know the severity of the situation.

Despite the fact that her older sister was with her at school and although James was nearby in Oxford, Jane was miserable at Mrs. Cawley's academy. The school was stiff and serious; the rigid structure was a drastic change from the freedom of life in the country. Jane would later describe being dragged through "dismal chapels, dusty libraries and greasy halls" when she thought about life in Oxford. In her novel *Mansfield Park*, Jane would detail the pain and unhappiness of 10-year-old Fanny Price, separated "from everybody she had been used to. Her feelings were very acute, and too little understood to be properly attended to. Nobody meant to be unkind, but nobody put themselves out of their way to secure her comfort."

The children at Mrs. Cawley's school lived with her, much as students did at Mr. Austen's school, and so when Mrs. Cawley decided to move to the southern coast town of Southampton, she simply relocated her school as well, taking her students with her. Southampton was closer to the Austen home; it was also a busy port full of soldiers dressed in handsome uniforms. Shortly after Mrs. Cawley and her pupils arrived at Southampton, the town was stricken with typhoid fever. Many in the town became ill and began dying, but Mrs. Cawley did not leave—nor, when Cassandra and Jane became sick, did she contact their parents. It was their cousin, Jane Cooper, also a student at the school, who ignored her teacher's instructions and wrote to her own mother, telling her that she and her cousins were very sick. Mrs. Cooper quickly arrived with Mrs. Austen. By then Jane was seriously ill; in the eighteenth century typhoid fever often proved fatal, especially to children.

Jane and Cassandra were cared for by their mother and soon able to return home. Jane Cooper also recovered. Sadly, her mother, who had hurried to Southampton to care for her daughter, caught typhoid fever herself and died.

The experience would mark Jane, and in her later writings she would criticize both the teaching profession and girls schools. In *Sense and Sensibility*, for example, she notes that Elinor and Marianne Dashwood are placed in the room of Charlotte Palmer, where "over the mantelpiece still hung a landscape in coloured silks of her performance, in proof of her having spent seven years at a great school in town to some effect."

The girls spent a few months at home, where an artist was hired to teach them how to draw portraits. Jane found the detailed work frustrating, and she showed little skill for drawing. Soon, though, her parents decided that the girls needed more formal teaching. So, they were sent away once more—again with their cousin Jane Cooper—this time to Reading, outside London, to attend the Abbey School, so named because it was built on the ruins of a medieval monastery.

While there were several boarding schools for girls, formal education for girls was fairly uncommon. Most of the expectations and expenses surrounding education were focused on the boys in a family. Boys attended grammar or public schools and then went on to the only two universities in England—Cambridge or Oxford. Those who attended these universities, usually only a few hundred students at a time, were expected to become clergymen or attorneys, or if they were quite wealthy, to manage their estates and property. Only the very wealthy hired private tutors or governesses. Many children were taught by their parents or had no education at all.

Jane's father did not feel qualified to teach his daughters. So in 1784 they traveled to a different school to be taught by Miss Sarah Hackett, who called herself "Mrs. Latournelle." Mrs. Latournelle described herself as a French teacher, although she could not speak a single word of French.

In fact, the girls learned little at the Abbey School. Mrs. Latournelle, a large woman with an artificial leg made out of cork, believed that it was more important for girls to be happy than to actually be taught anything. She did little work herself and absolutely none in the afternoons. After lunch she left the girls alone to entertain themselves. She spent the rest of the day giving orders: for clothes to be washed, for meals to be prepared, or for tea to be served.

The girls spent a good part of the day gossiping, speculating on how Mrs. Latournelle lost her leg, or telling ghost stories about the ancient ruins on which the school had been built.

The body of King Henry I was buried near the school, and it was rumored that the ghosts of two young children haunted the place where the monastery once stood. During Jane's first year at the school, a shriveled human hand was discovered in the ruins, and soon after yet another bit of human remains— a skeleton—was discovered behind the Abbey's walls. These sparked wildly inventive horror stories with which the girls frightened each other.

At the Abbey School, three assistants were hired to do the actual teaching, and Jane and her sister were given some instruction in the skills thought necessary for young ladies: French, music, drawing, writing, spelling, dancing, and needlework. These lessons lasted no more than two or three hours a day; the remainder of the day was free for the girls to do as they wished.

Jane may have been thinking of the Abbey School when she described the school of Mrs. Goddard in *Emma* as "a real, honest, old-fashioned boarding school, where a reasonable quantity of accomplishments were sold at a reasonable price, and where girls might be sent to be out of the way, and scramble themselves into a little education, without any danger of coming back prodigies." Jane and Cassandra enjoyed the lazy atmosphere of the school, and wrote home enthusiastically after their brother Edward and Jane Cooper's brother (also named Edward) arrived at the school and were allowed to take the girls to dinner at the most fashionable inn in Reading.

A short while after the news of this rather shocking trip reached home, Mr. Austen began to consider the cost of the school and the value of its education. It was costing him the same price (35 pounds per student per year) to educate his daughters as he charged his own students, and he suspected that the education they were receiving was considerably less than he was giving his students. He was concerned that fancy dinners at elegant hotels might not be the best entertainment for ten- and twelve-year-old girls.

Toward the end of 1786, both girls were pulled from the Abbey School and returned home. Jane celebrated her eleventh birthday at Steventon. Her formal education was over, and she would never again venture far away from her family.

Marie Antoinette was the queen of France in the late 1700s, and was one of the many cosmopolitan topics that Austen's cousin Eliza Hancock related to her when she arrived in Steventon in 1786. Eliza was twenty-five years old, and her stories of high society life and travel abroad fascinated Austen.

3

Family Life

JANE HAD ENJOYED the Abbey School, but was happy to be home again in Steventon. Once more she could enjoy long walks along the winding roads that dotted the village or through the fields where the Austens grew potatoes and raised their livestock. The house had a formal garden with a sundial and strawberry beds, and the fields were lined by double rows of shrubs that marked off their property, as well as the properties of their neighbors. Wildflowers lined the path to the church, and chestnut, fir and elm trees grew along one side of the Austen home.

Guests frequently visited the rectory, and in December 1786, shortly after Jane's eleventh birthday, her cousin Eliza Hancock arrived. Eliza had also celebrated a birthday in December, turning twenty-five, but she was now a French countess, known as the Comtesse de Feuillide. Joining her were her mother, named Philadelphia, and her six-month-old baby, Hastings François Louis Eugène Capot de Feuillide. Jane had heard many family stories about her cousin Eliza, but she had been living abroad since Jane was a baby.

Her arrival caused great excitement in the family. Eliza talked of Marie Antoinette, the beautiful French queen. She shared stories of her glamorous life in London, where she and her mother had rented a house and where they traveled about in a coach pulled by four horses. She talked of going to court, visiting with duchesses, and nights spent in elegant entertainment that lasted until five in the morning. She was dressed in the latest French fashions and had a French maid, and every day she played music on a pianoforte (a smaller and softer version of a modern piano) that the Austens had borrowed for her to use.

Eliza's life made her as dramatic a character as the heroines in the novels Jane was reading. As a child, Eliza had enjoyed an expensive and fashionable home in London. Her father— or at least the man who she believed was her father—was considerably older than her mother, and was away in India during most of her childhood before dying when she was thirteen. Her godfather settled a small fortune on her and, when she turned fifteen, her mother took her to Europe, where she traveled to Germany, Belgium, and then on to Paris. Soon she was meeting Marie Antoinette and writing letters describing her attendance at the theater and at the new opera house.

At nineteen, she married a French officer who was 11 years older and was quite handsome but had no title, despite her claims to have become a countess as a result of the marriage.

Her husband enjoyed a lavish and expensive lifestyle, and quickly spent all of his own money and set to work spending hers as well. At the time of Eliza's visit, he was working in southern France and building a mansion there for his family. It was at his suggestion that Eliza had traveled north to England, as he had wanted his child to be born in that country.

Eliza's tales of adventure and travel fascinated Jane, and her Christmas visit of 1786 was a happy time for the family. Only two of the Austen boys were at home—fifteen-year-old Henry and twelve-year-old Charles, known by the family as "Fly." The oldest, James, was traveling to France to visit Eliza's husband. Edward, now adopted by the wealthy Knights, was traveling through Europe—doing the "Grand Tour," as many wealthy English gentlemen did when completing their education. Francis, hoping for a career in the navy, was attending a naval school at Portsmouth and would only be at home for a short visit.

Eliza, having spread a bit of her glamour over the family, returned to her home in London after receiving a promise that Henry (who was had developed a serious crush on her) would be allowed to visit in a few months' time. Mr. Austen's students returned from their Christmas holiday, and life for the family settled once more into noisy, busy routine.

Mr. Austen had believed that the half-hearted education offered at Abbey School could just as easily—and much less expensively—be replicated at home, and although there were special instructors available to give them lessons in piano and drawing, he seemed to have depended upon Cassandra and Jane to learn and study on their own. Many different types of books were available, and the girls were encouraged to read whatever and whenever they chose. Jane read classical literature, history and poetry, as well as contemporary authors, and knew both French and a little Italian.

She was allowed to read the two types of novels most popular in the eighteenth century: sentimental novels, in which an idealized hero and heroine were separated for one reason or another but overcame the obstacle to their happiness in the end; and horror novels (or, as they were referred to then, "novels of terror"), where in a setting of haunted castles a villain would threaten the safety and virtue of a beautiful girl. Jane enjoyed reading the works of Henry Fielding, Samuel Richardson, and Dr. Samuel Johnson, and the poetry of William Cowper. Jane would later complain of her own lack of education, but she certainly acquired a great skill in expressing herself with a style that was both entertaining and

Did you know...

Austen's relatives were her first audience, and she valued their comments even after she became a published author. She noted their reactions to *Mansfield Park* after its publication in 1814:

Mr. K [Edward Austen Knight]: Not so clever as P.&P. [*Pride and Prejudice*] . . .

My Mother: Not liked it so well as P.&P. Thought Fanny insipid . . .

Cassandra: Thought it quite as clever, tho' not so brilliant, as P.&P. . . . .

My Eldest Brother: A warm admirer of it in general . . .

FWA [Francis William Austen]: We certainly do not think it as a whole, equal to P.&P. — but it has many & great beauties. . . . .

grammatically correct. All that she read would shape her own writing.

The family also enjoyed the habit of reading aloud to each other. In the mid-eighteenth century, reading aloud was viewed as a special skill, and it took talent to properly read dialogue, poetry, and prose with the correct expressions and pauses. Later in life, Jane would complain that her mother showed little skill in reading aloud from Jane's own writing, but her father was more accomplished and enjoyed reading many different styles of writing. This certainly influenced Jane's later novels; the experience of listening to dialogue and descriptions read aloud would have sharpened Jane's understanding of what worked and what did not.

In *Sense and Sensibility*, Jane noted how the ability—or lack thereof—to read aloud (in this case, the poetry of Cowper) could shape impressions. Marianne, the more sensitive and emotional sister, criticizes the young man her older sister Elinor admires—Edward Ferrars—for his unsuccessful attempt to adequately read to the group:

> "O mamma! How spiritless, how tame was Edward's manner in reading to us last night! I felt for my sister most severely. Yet she bore it with so much composure, she seemed scarcely to notice it. I could hardly keep my seat. To hear those beautiful lines which have frequently almost driven me wild, pronounced with such impenetrable calmness, such dreadful indifference!"

Jane also learned the art of elegant writing, considered an important skill for young women. A lady had to be able to write clearly and neatly using the only type of pen available—a quill pen—and also to develop a small handwriting style to save money on paper and postage.

One of the earliest descriptions of Jane Austen comes from her cousin Phila Walter, given following a visit the

Austens made to Kent in the summer of 1788. They had traveled to Kent for a vacation and, while there, visited their elderly great-uncle Francis. At a dinner hosted for the family, Phila Walter (then in her twenties) found her twelve-year-old cousin to be much less pleasing than her older sister, Cassandra. Jane was quiet, shy, tall, and slim, but already developing an eye for the absurd in the behavior around her. Whether she smiled once too often at Phila's comments or made a few jokes at Phila's expense is uncertain, but it is clear that Phila found Jane to be unusual and not in a good way. Writing after the dinner to cousin Eliza, Phila described Jane as "whimsical and affected," "not at all pretty," and "very prim."

Eliza did not share Phila's critical and unkind assessment of Jane. Several years later, in a letter to Phila, she would describe both Cassandra and sixteen-year-old Jane as beauties who "are I think equally sensible, and both so to a degree seldom met with, but still my heart gives the preference to Jane."

Jane's position as the seventh child in a family of eight children, in addition to various male students, meant that she frequently needed to compete for her parent's attention. Jane's voice would eventually be heard in her ability to write stories and plays.

Jane's family was full of clever, accomplished people. Francis had successfully completed naval school with honors, and at the end of 1788, the fifteen-year-old returned home briefly before leaving for his first commission—a trip to the East Indies. His father wrote him a loving letter, full of advice and a surprising level of respect, noting the importance of compliant, good-humored behavior as well as faithful prayer, and concluding with a heartfelt wish: "I have nothing more to add but my blessing and best prayers for your health and prosperity, and to beg you would never forget you have

The Vyne Manor House in Hampshire was just one of the places that hosted parties and gatherings attended by Austen and her sisters. Many of these experiences would inspire similar scenes in Austen's novels. It was also at this time that Austen began writing in earnest into notebooks.

not upon earth a more disinterested and warm friend than your truly affectionate father, Geo Austen." The letter meant so much to Francis that he carried it with him wherever he went. It was discovered among his belongings when he died, 76 years later, at the age of 91.

Francis' naval tour would keep him from home for five years. Jane, Cassandra, and Charles remained at home, with frequent visits from James and Henry during academic breaks from Oxford. That Christmas the family performed two plays, *The Sultan* and *High Life Below Stairs,* with Jane taking leading roles, most often opposite her brother, Henry.

The family enjoyed an active social life. There were frequent parties in the neighborhood and visitors arrived often to spend time with the Austens. Much of the material Jane would later use in her early novels—her astute observations of society and its customs—came from her experiences during this time at Steventon. She and Cassandra attended dances at some of the more elegant, large homes nearby. Some of these homes still remain, and visitors to the Vyne, near Basingstoke, or to Barclays Bank in the Market Place in Basingstoke (once the Assembly Rooms), may get a sense of the elegant settings where Jane and her sister enjoyed parties and dancing. Jane and Cassandra also visited their relatives: the Coopers in Bath and the Leigh Perrots at their country home in Berkshire. These visits gave Jane additional future material in the opportunity to observe life in a more sophisticated setting and the people that lived there.

At the time, it was James who was viewed as the writer of the family. He had become a writer of poetry, and in early 1789 he began to publish a weekly magazine called *The Loiterer*. James wrote the majority of the magazine's articles himself, edited the contributions of others, and distributed the magazine, at a cost of three pence, to readers in London, Oxford, Birmingham, Bath, and Reading.

During the fourteen months that *The Loiterer* was published, Jane was also writing. She began putting some of her pieces into a notebook and labeled one of these *History of England* ("by a partial, prejudiced, & ignorant Historian"). Jane's *History* was, more accurately, a comical history of matters of interest to the Austen family, and sketches and word games designed to be read aloud. The end of the *History* carries the date Nov. 26, 1791, indicating that it was completed just before Jane turned sixteen.

In a second notebook, Jane copied a story that she titled *Lesley Castle*. *Lesley Castle* was a comic novel, told in letters, and the maturity of its writing and the strength of each of the characters' voices shows how rapidly Jane's talent was developing. The story contains some surprising themes for the sixteen-year-old daughter of a clergyman: a young mother who abandons her baby and runs away with a man who was not her husband; her husband's conversion to Catholicism so that their marriage may be annulled; and happy remarriages. Jane's father recognized her talent and supported her writing, purchasing the expensive notebooks and paper she needed.

Jane's writing, even as a teenager, shows clear signs of how closely she studied the people she encountered, how sharply and quickly she could assess their strengths and weaknesses, and how she could turn silliness into comedy. From one of her earliest notebooks came this description:

> All her stock of knowledge was exhausted in a very few Days, and when Kitty had learnt from her, how large their house in Town was, when the fashionable Amusements began, who were the celebrated Beauties and who the best Milliner, Camilla had nothing further to teach, except the Characters of any of her Acquaintance, as they occurred in Conversation; which was done with equal Ease and Brevity, by saying that the person was either the sweetest Creature in the world, and one of whom she was dotingly fond, or horrid, shocking and not fit to be seen.

Jane's earliest writing was done to amuse her family and friends. Most of her sketches were meant to be read aloud, and in some instances they were written for—and dedicated to—a particular member of her family or friend. She was fortunate to grow up in a family whose members enjoyed reading and writing and who gave her time and space to write without demanding too much of her.

A wedding scene in the 1995 film of Austen's Sense and Sensibility, *directed by Ang Lee and starring Emma Thompson and Hugh Grant. After Austen had turned sixteen, she attended the weddings of family members, inspiring her own thoughts on marriage which would be revealed through characters in her books.*

4

A Time of Change

IN THE LATE eighteenth century, young ladies were expected to take their place in society (or "come out," as the transition was then described) at around the age of sixteen. Jane was no exception, although by this time she had clearly demonstrated her talent for writing. Her days were spent in fairly typical ways for a young woman of her position: she helped her mother with housework; did needlework; read; went for long walks; had occasional lessons in music, drawing, and dance; and visited friends and neighbors. Once Jane joined society by "coming out," she added to this list going to balls and dining out more formally. The goal for young ladies who came out was quite simple: to find an appropriate husband.

Jane's attractiveness was quite in style for her time. She was tall and slim, with dark, curly hair, bright hazel eyes, and lovely skin. She was graceful, and moved—whether walking or dancing (which she loved)—with style. She and her sister, Cassandra, had plenty of young men asking them to dance whenever they appeared at a ball.

In 1791, Jane's family circle was extended by the first of several weddings. In December 1791, Jane's brother Edward married the eighteen-year-old daughter of a wealthy baronet, Elizabeth Bridges. His adoptive family, the Knights, provided the young couple with a lovely home called Rowlings in Kent, and Jane and Cassandra visited there often. The following year, James—who had been ordained as a clergy-man and was serving as a curate near Steventon—married Anna Matthew, the daughter of wealthy neighbors who provided the newlyweds with a generous allowance that enabled them to live in a style higher than that of the ordinary young country curate.

That summer, yet another wedding took place—this one of Jane Cooper, who had remained a close friend to the Austen girls. Jane Cooper's father had died, and so she was married at Steventon to a captain in the Royal Navy.

All of these weddings had some influence on Jane Austen. Dreaming of her own wedding, she took a page from her father's parish register—the book that listed all of the births, deaths, and marriages in the community—and wrote down some fictitious names of the man who might one day become her husband. Her daydreams included "Edmund Arthur William Mortimer, of Liverpool," "Henry Frederick Howard Fitzwilliam, of London," and the much less grand "Jack Smith."

At the same time that the Austens at Steventon were busying themselves with multiple weddings, their relatives were dealing with more serious matters. Jane's aunt, Philadelphia Hancock, was battling breast cancer. Her daughter Eliza was with her, and lacking modern knowledge or medicine, they attempted multiple promised "miracle cures" as Philadelphia's pain increased.

Eliza's son, Hastings, was causing equal sorrow. It was clear by now that he was failing to develop normally. Eliza has taken the unusual step, for those days, of dressing her young son in pants in the hope that it would help him stand and walk more easily, but the method had not worked. Meanwhile, Eliza's husband was back in France. The year 1792 was a difficult time to be in France, particularly for a man like Jean Capot de Feuillide who owed his living to the royal family and so was a firm supporter of the king and queen at a time when revolution was beginning to break out. Eliza's husband was attacked by an angry mob of peasants who immediately rummaged through his new home. He was lucky to escape with his life and hurried to Paris, where he thought a royalist might be a bit safer.

Philadelphia Hancock died in February 1792. Eliza's husband was able to travel to England for the funeral, but knowing that his property would be seized if he remained out of the country, he soon returned to Paris.

A few months later, Eliza and her son traveled to Steventon, where they remained for several months. Jane enjoyed Eliza's company, and the whole house enjoyed caring for Hastings. Apart from Mr. Austen's students, there were no other boys in the house; Charles, at twelve, was attending the Portsmouth naval school, just as Francis had, and Francis himself was still away in the East Indies.

In 1793, the first Austen grandchildren were born. Jane

became an aunt to Fanny (Edward's daughter) and Anna (James' daughter). Later, after being away two years, Francis finally returned home after being made a lieutenant.

In February of 1793, war broke out between England and France. Henry, who had been studying to be a clergyman at Oxford, now decided to join the Oxfordshire Militia. The war proved a help to Henry, who found himself well suited to military life and to the travel it involved. He would remain an officer for the next seven years, receiving several promotions.

The war would prove a much greater hardship to Eliza. The French Revolution was now fully formed, and angry mobs were raging through the streets of Paris. Eliza's husband, known to be a sympathizer with the king and queen, was seized. On February 22, 1794, he was condemned to death by guillotine. He was beheaded only a few hours later.

Eliza remained with the Austens for several months, as they did their best to comfort the young woman who suddenly found herself penniless (the revolutionary forces had seized her estate) and a widow. By summer, she was ready to travel north to stay with other friends, although she and Jane exchanged frequent letters.

Jane also spent the summer of 1794 traveling. She and Cassandra were sought-after guests, being intelligent, attractive young women who enjoyed dancing, and thus were a happy addition to the tea parties and balls to which they were invited. They also traveled to Kent, where Edward's family now included a son also named Edward.

By now, Cassandra had fallen in love with Thomas Fowle, a young man who was eight years older. He had been one of her father's students, living with the family until Cassandra was about ten, and was also a friend of James. He had become a clergyman and had performed the wedding of Jane Cooper when Cassandra was nineteen. It was probably at

A scene depicting some of the chaos of the French Revolution, which affected Austen directly. Her cousin Eliza came to live with the Austens after her husband, a sympathizer to the king and queen of France, was beheaded.

that time that he proposed to Cassandra, but the engagement was never officially announced. While both families were quite pleased with the engagement, Thomas Fowle's income as a clergyman was quite small. He had been promised a large parish in Shropshire as soon as it was available—in other words, as soon as the clergyman there died or retired. So Thomas and Cassandra decided to wait to marry until his income could better support a wife.

Jane had followed in Cassandra's footsteps many times over the years, so it is not surprising that when Cassandra became engaged, Jane determined that she should, too. While visiting Edward in Kent, she attracted the attention of her brother's neighbor, Edward Taylor. Jane quickly decided that she was in love with him, but marriages were frequently decided with financial motives in mind, and potential spouses were evaluated based on their assets and income. Edward Taylor was seeking a wife with slightly more assets than Jane could provide, and the relationship never grew into something more than a flirtation.

Apparently, Jane flirted quite a bit that summer. In fact, Jane was described by one woman who met her at a ball in Basingstoke as "the prettiest, silliest, most affected husband hunting butterfly she ever remembered."

It is interesting to read what the more mature Jane thought of marriage, or at least wrote of marriage, in *Mansfield Park*:

> "With all due respect to such of the present company as chance to be married, my dear Mrs. Grant, there is not one in a hundred of either sex who is not taken in when they marry. Look where I will, I see that it is so; and I feel that it must be so, when I consider that it is, of all transactions, the one in which people expect most from others, and are least honest themselves."

Jane probably viewed the prospect of marriage a bit more kindly at the age of eighteen, when it was expected that she must marry.

For her nineteenth birthday, Jane's father presented her with a small, mahogany writing desk, complete with drawer for keeping supplies and a glass inkstand. It is possible that Mr. Austen was becoming a bit concerned at Jane's wild flirting and parties and, knowing how she loved to write, hoped that she would confine her passions to the written page until she could meet the right sort of young man.

If Mr. Austen hoped to turn Jane away from flirting, he met with mixed success. She did soon begin writing a new story, but *Lady Susan*, as the short novel was called, focused on the adventures of a woman who boasted of herself as "the most accomplished coquette [flirt] in England."

Once again, Jane focused on telling her story through letters. Lady Susan, the novel's heroine, tells her own story, gleefully relating her successes at charming nearly every man she meets, whether married or not. The adventures of this admittedly wicked woman and bad mother are told with such an entertaining style that she ultimately becomes a sympathetic heroine. It is, in essence, the story of a woman much more clever, much stronger, than any of the people around her.

Lady Susan is quite different from the writing that would follow. It is possible that her family was slightly shocked by its almost cheerful views of adultery and betrayal. *Lady Susan*, although never discarded, was put aside until, about ten years later, Jane copied it from her notebook. She never attempted to have it published, and the novels that followed it would contain heroines who were, if equally strong and clever, quite a bit less wicked.

In 1795, Cassandra's fiancé Thomas Fowle was invited to join his patron, the Earl of Craven, on a voyage to the West Indies. The parish that Lord Craven had promised him was not yet available; Lord Craven, a soldier, was taking his regiment to the West Indies, where the French were trying to spark a rebellion against British rule. He suggested that Thomas Fowle come with him to serve as his private chaplain.

It was not an easy decision. Fowle's wedding to Cassandra has already been postponed several times. The long voyage to the West Indies would mean yet another delay. Fowle wanted to maintain a good relationships with Lord Craven and ultimately agreed to accompany him, quickly writing his will (in which he left 1,000 pounds to Cassandra and his property to his father) before departing.

As Cassandra settled down to wait for her fiancé's return, the family encountered tragedy. James' wife, Anne, unexpectedly and suddenly died, leaving their two-year-old daughter,

Anna, to wander the house sadly calling for her mother. James decided to send the little girl to Steventon, where she quickly attached herself to her Aunt Jane. Jane spent long hours making up stories for her niece, and soon she was beginning to work on a story for an older audience. She was sketching out ideas for another novel, one about two sisters—one sensible and wise, the other impatient and romantic. The novel, written in the form of letters between the two sisters, would be called *Elinor and Marianne*, but it would eventually be revised and retitled *Sense and Sensibility*.

In January 1796, Jane wrote to Cassandra, who was then visiting her future in-laws, the Fowles, in Berkshire. Jane told her sister about a ball she attended where she danced with someone new to the neighborhood—a handsome, intelligent and charming Irishman named Tom Lefroy. Tom visited Jane at her home the next day, as it was the custom

Did you know...

Money and marriage are linked in many of Austen's novels. Money—or its lack thereof—frequently influences her characters' decisions about choosing one person over another as a potential spouse. Marriage was viewed as a linking of two families. Grooms would offer up a certain income; brides would frequently have a fixed sum of money "settled" on them by a parent or relative. This "settlement" was a legal document that specified that the money or property a bride brought into a marriage would remain hers, and might include mention of how that would then pass on to her children.

for young men to visit with their dance partners the day after a dance. Jane's letter to Cassandra described his appearance and clothing in detail, and made it clear that she was quite infatuated. She even revealed that she and Lefroy had talked about the novel *Tom Jones*—Fielding's novel was considered a bit shocking for its time, and by telling her sister that they had discussed it, Jane's letter revealed that their conversation had been a bit bold.

Lefroy returned Jane's interest—perhaps too obviously. His family needed him to make a good marriage, but not to a poor clergyman's daughter, but rather to a wealthy young woman who could help support him and his family. Sensing the growing attraction between the two, Lefroy's parents quickly sent him away to London. It was a sad disappointment to Jane. She would not hear of him again for three years and then only from her father who had encountered Lefroy's mother and asked about her son.

Lefroy eventually married an heiress—the wealthy sister of a college friend—settled in Ireland and became a successful lawyer. He served as a Member of Parliament and ultimately was appointed Lord Chief Justice of Ireland in 1852. By then, the young woman who had written to her sister of her romance with him was dead. It would have pleased her to know, however, that Lefroy never forgot her. As an old man, he admitted to a nephew that he was in love with her, although he described it as a "boyish love."

Jane would also remember the short-lived romance with Tom Lefroy. Her experience of thwarted love, of the sudden arrival of a handsome stranger, the pain of his equally sudden departure, and her understanding of family disapproval and the disappointment it could bring would become themes that would appear in her novels again and again.

An 1811 engraving depicting Elinor Dashwood and Lucy Steele in a scene out of *Sense* and *Sensibility*. *Originally titled* Elinor *and* Marianne, *the novel was first written as a series of letters between the two sisters, but Austen soon scrapped the format in favor of a more conventional narrative.*

5

A Writing Life

A FEW MONTHS after Tom Lefroy's departure and the end of Jane's romance, her father decided that he would no longer teach students at Steventon. Suddenly, many of the tasks that had occupied much of Jane's time—assisting with the cooking, cleaning, and laundry for her family plus so many students— vanished, and she was left with more free time, and more privacy in which to enjoy it.

Much of this new free time was filled with writing. In October of 1796, Jane had begun work on *First Impressions*, the novel that would later be revised and retitled *Pride and Prejudice*. In about nine months' time, she had completed *First Impressions* and returned to the manuscript of *Elinor and Marianne*. She had become dissatisfied with the novel's structure, finding that telling the story through letters exchanged between the title characters was awkward, forcing her to constantly keep the sisters apart in order to advance the story. Instead, she decided to rewrite *Elinor and Marianne*, structuring it in a more straightforward narrative. Into the spring of 1798 she worked, revising, rewriting, and rethinking much of what she had earlier completed. Finally, she even changed the title, renaming this novel *Sense and Sensibility* (the title came from an essay that appeared in a magazine called *Lady's Monthly Museum*, to which Jane's mother subscribed).

Her revisions completed, she next began work on a new novel, one that would be titled *Susan*—and eventually retitled *Northanger Abbey*. In four years' time she would have completed work on three novels—all before she turned twenty-four.

Much of Jane's success in dialogue and comic situations was informed by her own realistic observations of the behavior around her. Despite the impressive amount of writing she did in four years, she did not do so in isolation, hidden away from the world while scribbling in solitary thought at her desk for months at a time. She traveled to visit family, she entertained friends and relatives, and she participated in the lives around her.

Her cousin Eliza had provided much entertainment for the Austen family over the years, and during one visit to the rectory Eliza had decided that she would marry Jane's widower brother, James. She enjoyed the country spring, and she seemed truly to believe that she could leave behind the sophisticated life she enjoyed in London and settle down to life as a country clergyman's wife. Though James did propose, Eliza wavered before finally realizing that she could not settle down to a quiet parish life.

It is tempting for readers of *Mansfield Park* to see bits of Eliza in the character of Mary Crawford, who early in the novel offers the following opinion of churchgoing:

> It is safer to leave people to their own devices on such subjects. Everybody likes to go their own way—to choose their own time and manner of devotion. The obligation of attendance, the formality, the restraint, the length of time— altogether it is a formidable thing, and what nobody likes; and if the good people who used to kneel and gape in that gallery could have foreseen that the time would ever come when men and women might lie another ten minutes in bed when they woke with a headache, without danger of repro- bation because chapel was missed, they would have jumped with joy and envy.

When Mary Crawford discovers that the man to whom she has offered this opinion, Edmund Bertram, is in fact planning to become a clergyman, she is slightly embarrassed—but only slightly. Still later, having successfully made Edmund fall in love with her, but being unsuccessful in her attempt to persuade him to choose another line of work, she debates whether or not she might accept his proposal and become the wife of a country clergyman, leaving behind the social whirl of London and a life of greater financial comfort. She finally decides that it is, after all, too great a sacrifice, and agrees only to one last dance with Edmund before he takes his orders because, as she tells him, "she has never danced with a clergyman and she never *will*."

Curiously, there are also traces of Eliza in another character in *Mansfield Park*: Mary Crawford's brother, Henry Crawford, who delights in flirting first with one Bertram sister, then the other, sparking intense jealousy and competition between the two young women before moving on to their cousin. Eliza, too, delighted in sparking jealousy between two brothers—in this case, Jane's brothers James and Henry, both of whom at various points fell in love with her.

James, rejected by Eliza, quickly selected another woman to be his bride—a friend of the Austen family named Mary Lloyd, who had been visiting at Steventon. Jane's mother was quite relieved at the choice of the more sensible Mary over her wild niece, and she quickly wrote to Mary expressing her enthusiasm: "I look forward to you as a real comfort in my old age, when Cassandra is gone into Shropshire & Jane—the Lord knows where."

However, Mrs. Austen's plans for Cassandra would soon be forced to change, for she would not move to Shropshire and become Mrs. Thomas Fowle. Cassandra had been expecting her fiancé to return from the West Indies in the spring of 1797, but in April she learned that, two months earlier he had caught yellow fever. The disease proved fatal, and he was buried at sea.

It was a devastating blow to Cassandra. She had decided to wait for marriage, had kept her two-year engagement private, and now her plans had been shattered. Jane was astonished at her sister's ability to mourn privately and to keep her emotions largely under control. She was working at the time on the novel that would become *Sense and Sensibility*, and it is likely that the remarkable self-control that Elinor Dashwood exercises when her prospects for happiness seem to have been dissolved was influenced by Jane's observations of Cassandra's ability to remain composed after such a blow.

A scene from the 1999 film adaptation of Mansfield Park. *Austen's cousin Eliza Hancock had an influence on Austen, and many believe that Eliza's own personality is present in some characters in Mansfield Park, including those of Mary Crawford and Henry Crawford.*

In later years, Cassandra found meaning in this passage from another of Jane's novels, *Persuasion*:

> How eloquent could Anne Elliot have been,—how eloquent, at least, were her wishes on the side of early warm attachment, and a cheerful confidence in futurity, against that over-anxious caution which seems to insult exertion and distrust Providence!—She had been forced into prudence in her youth, she learned romance as she grew older—the natural sequel of an unnatural beginning.

Cassandra marked this passage and wrote; "Dear dear Jane! This deserves to be written in letters of gold."

It was not only Cassandra who treasured Jane's writing. Jane's father was certainly sufficiently impressed by the completed *First Impressions* to submit it in November 1797 to the respected London publishing company of Thomas Cadell. He did not indicate who the author was, nor his relationship to her, but offered his compliments to the quality of work Cadell had published over the years and then noted that he was in possession of "a Manuscript Novel, comprised in three Vols. About the length of Miss Burney's *Evelina*." He then asked what the author would be expected to pay to publish it (as was common practice at that time) and "what you will venture to advance for the Property of it, if on a perusal, it is approved of?"

The novel was swiftly returned, marked "Declined by Return of Post." Whether or not Jane was aware of her father's attempt is not clear; she later reworked this novel into *Pride and Prejudice*. This manuscript that had been so quickly rejected would become one of the classics of English literature.

Because Jane had never written an autobiography, the majority of the family history gathered from this time is based on letters, particularly letters exchanged between Jane and Cassandra. Cassandra saved most of the correspondence, but selectively destroyed certain of the letters that she felt might reflect unfavorably on Jane or other family members. Many of these letters came from the period between the late 1790s and the early 1800s, and some may have had references to the death of Cassandra's fiancé.

It was another wedding that soon occupied the Austen family—on December 31, 1797, cousin Eliza married Jane's brother, Henry. Eliza had flirted with Henry, who was 10 years younger, for many years. At one point, he had briefly been engaged to another woman, but the engagement had been broken off. The romance between Eliza and Henry had rekindled when they met in May of 1797 in London; they met again in the fall when Henry's regiment was stationed in East Anglia and Eliza had traveled there to give her son some time by the sea (the doctors believed swimming in the sea might be good for him). The wedding apparently happened rather suddenly, and the newlyweds, with Hastings in tow, traveled to Ipswich where Eliza was warmly welcomed by Henry's regiment with parties and dances. The war with France was still going on, but Eliza had hopes that the revolutionary government would eventually be overthrown and her fortune restored, as Henry's income was not quite sufficient to support her lavish lifestyle.

With three of her brothers now married, Jane traveled frequently to visit them. She most often spent summers visiting Edward and his family in Kent. She traveled to his

Did you know...

The town of Bath was famous as a health resort and a popular choice for retirees during Jane Austen's time, due to the benefits many believed came from bathing in its ancient Roman thermal springs. Bath had been a fashionable destination during the early part of the eighteenth century, but by the time Austen visited there, it no longer enjoyed the same cachet. Her parents were married there, Austen lived there from 1801 to 1806, and her father was buried there. Bath plays an important role in the novels *Northanger Abbey* and *Persuasion*, and is referred to in *Mansfield Park*.

comfortable home in the summers of 1794, 1796, and 1798. By 1798, Edward and Elizabeth had four children—one daughter and three sons—and were expecting another. They had moved from their home at Rowlings to the much larger home that had belonged to the Knights called Godmersham. The home was located between Ashford and Canterbury, and was surrounded by a park where deer grazed and game could be hunted.

Jane was astonished at the size and scope of the grounds. The home itself had marble floors and a huge central building with two newer wings, one containing the kitchens, the other containing a large library with two fireplaces, five tables, and twenty-eight chairs. Guests could swim or boat on the nearby river; there were walled gardens, an orchard, and even an icehouse—a luxury for the late eighteenth century.

All of the Austens visited Godmersham at one time or another. Jane was treated kindly, but there was little doubt that she was a bit out of her element surrounded by such splendor and felt very much like a poor relation. Edward's daughter Fanny, who was very fond of her Aunt Jane, still remembered into her seventies that Jane had struggled to blend into the society of Godmersham:

> [she] was not so refined as she ought to have been from her talent... They [the Austens] were not rich & the people around with whom they chiefly mixed, were not at all high bred, or in short anything more than mediocre & they of course tho' superior in mental powers & cultivation were on the same level as far as refinement goes... Aunt Jane was too clever not to put aside all possible signs of "common-ness" (if such an expression is allowable) & teach herself to be more refined . . . Both the Aunts [Cassandra and Jane] were brought up in the

most complete ignorance of the World & its ways (I mean as to fashion &c) & if it had not been for Papa's marriage which brought them into Kent... they would have been, tho' not less clever & agreeable in themselves, very much below par as to good Society & its ways.

This seems quite a harsh criticism of a beloved aunt, but what we may interpret as snobbishness does in fact provide a useful illustration of what Jane must have experienced during visits with her brother Edward. She was far too sensitive and observant to have been unaware of how she was regarded by the others there. In understanding her sometimes harsh descriptions of the rigid social behavior of her time, it is important to keep in mind her own experiences during the period in which she was first writing her novels. These experiences would have emphasized that no matter how clever or witty young women may be, their intelligence mattered much less than their family connections and income.

During her visits to Godmersham, Jane made only one real friend—the children's governess, Anne Sharp. "Miss Sharp" (as Jane called her) enjoyed writing—she even wrote a play for the children to perform, and was smart and funny. Edward's family, of course, did not view her as an equal but rather as an employee, and perhaps this helped deepen the friendship. The two exchanged frequent letters and kept up a lifelong friendship, even after Anne Sharp left Godmersham in 1806 to set up and run her own boarding school in northern England.

When the Austens returned from Godmersham in 1798, Mrs. Austen quickly became ill and spent the next five weeks in bed. Cassandra had remained at Godmersham to help care for the new baby that had been born during their visit, and so it fell to Jane to care for her mother and assume the responsibility of running the household. She wrote to Cassandra of her experiments in planning out the menus and of her mother's continuous complaints about her health. Another letter contained the news that a baby had been born to James and Mary, a son named James-Edward.

Jane was quickly infatuated by her new nephew, but she soon was writing a critical description of her sister-in-law, comparing her unfavorably to the much wealthier Elizabeth at Godmersham and finding her wanting in style and cleanliness: "Mary does not manage things in such a way as to make me want to lay in myself. She is not tidy enough in her appearance; she has no dressing-gown to sit up in; her curtains are all too thin, and things are not in that comfort and style about her which are necessary to make such a situation an enviable one."

It is clear that Jane is feeling a bit jealous of yet another family member who was happily married and now with a baby. She was twenty-two years old, not quite beyond the point at which she might marry, but certainly her possibilities were growing more limited. In the letters of this period, her tone grows sharper, as if she is sensing that the possibility of marriage and children is slipping away from her.

Much of her sarcasm was devoted to her mother's claims of sickness. While Cassandra enjoyed the comforts of life at Godmersham, attending balls and dining in style, Jane was left to cope with her mother's symptoms that ranged from asthma, dropsy, water in her chest, and liver disorder to gouty swelling and discomfort in her ankles. Jane soon learned from Cassandra that her brother, Edward, was also ill and shared many of her mother's unusual symptoms. His solution was to go to Bath—the resort town whose waters were thought to be therapeutic—and he invited Jane and his mother to go with him.

By May 1779, Jane and her mother began the trip west to Bath. Jane was at work on another novel, *Northanger Abbey*, a novel whose central action takes place in the very town where Jane would soon find herself.

Visits to Bath were a frequent part of the Austen travels. Jane's uncle, the wealthy James Leigh-Perrot, and his wife had invited them to his home in Bath. The lovely architecture and presumed medicinal benefits of the waters (rumored since Roman times to be particularly healthful) had attracted crowds for many years. It was a sophisticated, cosmopolitan setting, complete with well-stocked libraries, fashionable people, and concerts and theater.

Edward had rented a fashionable, stately home for their visit, and once the family had arrived, he quickly began the trendy round of treatments—drinking and bathing in the waters, and testing out the new "electrical" cure, involving the use of electricity either via a "flesh-brush" or by provoking a spark—both thought to be curative. The treatments, however, were apparently unsuccessful, as Edward's health continued to pose problems.

Jane spent her days visiting and doing some shopping. After five weeks, the family returned to Steventon for a brief visit and then went on to Godmersham. Jane's mother, enjoying her travels, wanted them to continue, and persuaded Jane to accompany her on several additional visits to relatives in Adlestrop, Harpsden, and Surrey. Jane reluctantly agreed. While they were traveling, word reached them of a troubling incident involving their relatives in Bath, the Leigh-Perrots.

Mrs. Leigh-Perrot had visited a small shop called

Austen would frequently travel to Bath, England, where the waters in the Roman baths were thought to have therapeutic and curative properties. The location would figure prominently in her books Northanger Abbey *and* Persuasion.

Smith's, where she had purchased some black lace. After she had made her purchase and left the shop, an assistant had hurried after her to ask if she had also taken some white lace. Mrs. Leigh-Perrot handed her purchase to the assistant, who opened the package that had been wrapped in the shop, and discovered that next to the card of black lace was another card, this one of white lace. Mrs. Leigh Perrot was then requested to provide her name and address; four days later a policeman appeared at her door with a warrant for her arrest.

This seemingly innocent mistake quickly became a serious incident for the Leigh-Perrots. Because the lace had a value higher than a shilling, its theft was classified as grand larceny, for which the death penalty could be invoked. Even if she were not sentenced to death, Mrs. Leigh-Perrot could have faced a lesser sentence—being deported to Australia for fourteen months.

Mrs. Leigh-Perrot was placed in prison awaiting trial. Prisons in those days were horrific, nightmarish settings, and the wealthy, middle-aged Mrs. Leigh-Perrot faced the prospect of sleeping in straw, and possibly sharing a cell with a murderer. She quickly befriended the jailer, who agreed to keep watch over her in his home instead. Her husband, in poor health, insisted on accompanying her. The filthy home, filled with noisy children, two dogs, and three cats, was not a much better setting for the couple. Mrs. Leigh-Perrot wrote a letter outlining their plight to the Austens:

My dearest Perrot with his sweet composure adds to my Philosophy; to be sure he bids fair to have his patience tried in every way he can. Cleanliness has ever been his greatest delight and yet he sees the greasy toast laid by the dirty

Children on his Knees, and he feels the small Beer trickle down his sleeves on its way across the table unmoved. . . . Mrs. Scadding's knife, well licked to clean it from fried onions helps me now and then—you may believe how the Mess I am helped to is disposed of—here are two dogs and three Cats always full as hungry as myself.

Mrs. Austen, horrified by the conditions, quickly offered to send Jane and Cassandra to keep their aunt and uncle company. Mrs. Leigh-Perrot kindly refused, unwilling to see the two young ladies in such miserable conditions.

It soon became clear that Mrs. Leigh-Perrot had been the victim of a hoax. The item had been planted on her by the shopkeeper who, hoping to blackmail the Leigh-Perrots to avoid him pressing charges, had been disappointed when they refused and had decided to go ahead with his accusations. After spending the cold winter months in such horrible conditions, Mrs. Leigh-Perrot was relieved when the case finally went to trial on March 29, 1800.

Because of the Leigh-Perrot's status, the case had received considerable attention and the courtroom was crowded. After listening to several witnesses, Mrs. Leigh-Perrot herself took the stand and bravely explained that she would never hazard her reputation, nor endanger her husband's peace of mind and health, for such a trivial matter. Her speech moved many to tears. When the jury finally left the courtroom, they deliberated for less than ten minutes before returning with a verdict of "not guilty."

The Leigh-Perrots faced expenses of about 2,000 pounds for their legal defense and the cost of transporting, housing, and feeding those witnesses who had testified on her behalf.

Jane did not write directly about her aunt's imprisonment, but it is possible that she used some of her aunt's descriptions of the chaotic living conditions in the jailer's home when she described, in Mansfield Park, the "confinement, bad air, bad smells" of the home of Fanny Price's parents where dirt, noise, and chaos provided a daily contrast with the life Fanny had known before.

Bath Abbey in the center of Bath. In 1800, Austen's mother announced that in less than a week, the entire family would move from Steventon to Bath. The announcement caused Austen to faint from shock, but even more importantly, the move put a crimp on her writing output, which she did not resume until 1809.

6

Leaving Home

BY LATE 1800, Austen had settled into a comfortable routine. The trial of Mrs. Leigh-Perrot ended happily, and Austen had spent several months enjoying her home life and visiting friends. She was nearly twenty-five years old, she had written three novels, and her letters to Cassandra (who was once again visiting their brother at Godmersham) are full of cheerful accounts of balls, neighbors, and the improvements her father had been making to the rectory garden.

At the end of November, Austen traveled with a friend to Ibthorpe, where they spent a week before returning to Steventon.

When she arrived home, her mother suddenly delivered a startling announcement, almost as soon as she had walked in the door: "Well, girls, it is all settled; we have decided to leave Steventon in such a week and go to Bath." The news that her parents had so suddenly and unexpectedly decided to move was such a shock to Jane that she immediately fainted.

Beyond the fainting spell, there is no additional evidence that tells precisely what Austen felt immediately after hearing the news. Although Cassandra saved many letters that passed between her sister and herself in the weeks leading up to the news, there are none from November 30, 1800 to January 3, 1801, despite the fact that Cassandra remained at Godmersham throughout this time. It is impossible to believe that such a momentous decision went undiscussed between the two sisters; in the family memoir written by William Austen-Leigh and Richard Arthur Austen-Leigh, this is explained by the note: "according to the rule acted on by Cassandra, destruction of her sister's letters was a proof of their emotional interest."

Whatever the true emotions that the news sparked in Austen, by early January her correspondence with Cassandra indicated that she had resigned herself to the move, and in fact was busy discussing quite practically precisely what sort of home they might find in the more expensive town of Bath. A retired clergyman of modest means would find it difficult to afford the kind of fashionable home in which Austen and her mother had stayed during their last visit to Bath, thanks to her brother.

There were debates about exactly how many servants the new household could afford. Mrs. Austen had

determined that there should be at least two maids. Mr. Austen decided that all of the furniture, apart from the beds, must be sold, and soon visitors were arriving at the rectory to make offers for the various pieces of furniture. It was agreed that Austen's brother, James, and his wife Mary would move into the rectory once the Austens left, with James serving as the parish's curate after Mr. Austen was gone. In fact, Austen was annoyed at how quickly James began making plans for moving in, taking possession of some of the furniture, the family pictures, and even her father's horses.

The move from Steventon would mark an important change in Austen's habits. By the time she was twenty-five, she had written three strong and accomplished novels. For the next ten years, however, she would write little. It was not until the summer of 1809 that she would once more resume the steady output of writing that had marked her earlier years.

It seems clear from this that Austen's writing was not based on stimulating events around her. Life in Bath was certainly more sophisticated than it had been in Steventon, rich with eccentric characters and plenty of social gatherings. For Austen, though, her writing apparently depended more on the discipline of daily practice—of having a quiet place and tranquil setting where she could plot out the stories in her head, allow the characters to shape, and hear their voices without being overly influenced by daily demands. The move to Bath was exactly the wrong thing for her writing.

Austen and her mother were the first to arrive in Bath. Cassandra had left Godmersham and traveled to London to visit Henry and his wife, Eliza. On May 5, 1801,

Austen wrote rather gloomily to Cassandra of her earliest impressions of her new home:

> The first view of Bath in fine weather does not answer my expectations; I think I see more distinctly through rain. The sun was got behind everything, and the appearance of the place from the top of Kingsdown was all vapour, shadow, smoke, and confusion.

A few days later, after a round of parties and dinners, she still seemed discouraged with the people of Bath:

> Another stupid party last night; perhaps if larger they might be less intolerable, but here there were only just enough to make one card table, with six people to look on and talk nonsense to each other. . . . I cannot anyhow continue to find people agreeable; I respect Mrs. Chamberlayne for doing her hair well, but cannot feel a more tender sentiment. Miss Langley is like any other short girls, with a broad nose and wide mouth, fashionable dress and exposed bosom. Adm. Stanhope is a gentlemanlike man, but then his legs are too short and his tail too long.

Cassandra and her father joined Austen and her mother in June. For the next five years, Austen would live at Bath, but there would be few written records to explain her feelings or show how she spent that time. For nearly four years there are no letters at all between Austen and Cassandra.

While the family was living in Bath, much of the time was spent traveling. Mr. Austen was seventy, and once removed from the work and routine at Steventon, he discovered a new love for exploring. He particularly liked the coastal areas of Devon and Dorset, where Austen enjoyed walks along the sea. The family is thought to have visited Sidmouth in 1801, Dawlish and Teignmouth,

The Austens eventually settled into their home in Bath, No. 4 Sydney Place, in 1801. Although the social scene kept Austen busy, she wrote about how "stupid" the many parties she attended were, and was undoubtedly unhappy that her new surroundings did not give her the peace she needed for writing.

and Tenby and Barmouth in Wales, in 1802, and Carmouth and Lyme Regis in 1803. Austen and Cassandra added to this itinerary trips to see their brother at Godmersham in both 1802 and 1803 and a visit to Lyme Regis with Henry and Eliza in the summer of 1804.

It is perhaps not surprising, with all of these trips and the general upheaval of moving, that Austen found it difficult to establish a new routine for her writing. The home in which the family finally settled in the fall of 1801 was No. 4 Sydney Place, in the Bathwick section of Bath. It was a bit far from the center of town, but it was a newer home, with tall windows in the drawing room that overlooked Sydney Gardens, and a small garden in the back.

In late November, Austen and Cassandra traveled to Manydown to visit their old friends, Catherine and Alethea Bigg. Manydown was full of happy memories. Located in a lovely park of cedar and beech trees only six miles from Steventon, Manydown Park (the home of the Biggs) had been the setting where Austen had danced with Tom Lefroy, and as a girl had enjoyed Catherine and Althea's company many times in the stately mansion. Jane and Cassandra planned to spend a few weeks there, but within a week the visit ended.

The reason was Catherine and Alethea's younger brother, Harris. It is possible that the Biggs had invited the Austens hoping to make a match between Harris and Austen. Their brother, five years younger than Austen, had been away at school for several years. The transformation was surprising—Harris had grown from an awkward young boy with a stammer to a tall young man. The stammer still appeared when he grew nervous, and he was awkward and not terribly witty, but Harris would inherit a sizeable fortune and property upon the death of his father, and it seemed appropriate that he find a wife.

On the evening of December 2, 1802, Harris Bigg asked Austen to become his wife. She had not been expecting the proposal, but once it was made, she thought carefully. In only two more weeks, she would turn twenty-seven, which apparently was a significant age to her. In *Sense and Sensibility*, Marianne Dashwood suggests that at such an age, a woman had few prospects:

> "A woman of seven-and-twenty," said Marianne, after pausing a moment, "can never hope to feel or inspire affection again; and if her home be uncomfortable, or her fortune small, I can suppose that she might bring herself to submit to the offices of a nurse, for the sake of the provision and security of a wife."

The marriage would place Austen in charge of a large Hampshire house and estate, close to her childhood home and the home of her brother James. She would be able to help her parents, her sister, and even her brothers. She would have sisters-in-law who were already her friends. She accepted Harris' proposal.

Harris' family was overjoyed by the news, but at some point during the night, Austen regretted her decision. In the morning, she again met alone with Harris, and this time explained that she had thought the matter over and realized that, after all, she could not marry him. Her reasons are not clear, but somehow the benefits Harris offered—of security, considerable fortune, and close friends as family members—were not enough. Austen and Cassandra hastily packed their bags, said their embarrassed farewells, and then hurried to James' home at Steventon, where they explained what had happened and begged him to help them return to Bath.

Following the embarrassing and very brief engagement, Austen returned to Bath and was, after a long absence, interested in taking a fresh look at the manuscripts she had transported with her from Steventon to Bath. She pulled out the manuscript for the novel *Northanger Abbey* (which was at the time titled *Susan*) and began to rewrite it. Her brother Henry arranged for the manuscript to be sold to a London publisher, Richard Crosby, who paid 10 pounds for the rights to publish it.

The sale of *Susan* added to Austen's renewed vigor for writing, and she began work on a new novel, this one titled *The Watsons*. The manuscript is the most closely autobiographical of any of her works, and this may be the reason why she chose to never complete it. It told the story of four sisters in desperate situations—poor and unmarried with a dying father. The women grapple with unsatisfying marital prospects, and they frequently distrust and/or compete with each other.

As Austen was deciding how the father in *The Watsons* should die, real deaths of people she cared about began occurring, and this may also have contributed to her unwillingness to finish this novel. First, in 1801, came Eliza's son Hastings, who had lived to be fifteen. While coping with sadness surrounding the death of Hastings, Austen's father fell ill. He had been experiencing fevers throughout most of their stay in Bath. When he recovered, in early 1804, Austen's mother became ill.

Finally, after both parents had recovered, Austen's father determined to give up his lease on the house at Sydney Place, and the family spent several months along the coast, in Lyme, where they were joined by Eliza and Henry. The family grieved the loss of poor Hastings, and enjoyed walks along Lyme's cliffs.

In late October, the Austens returned to Bath, renting a home on the east side of the town, in Green Park Buildings. Shortly after Austen celebrated her twenty-ninth birthday, on January 19, 1805, her father once again suffered from the fevers that had been bothering him. Only two days later, he was dead.

Austen was faced with the sad task of informing her brothers of their father's death. Her brother Frank was at sea, and since her first letter to him was incorrectly addressed, she was forced to write the news yet again, informing him that their father's death had been sudden and relatively peaceful, writing, "Except the restlessness and confusion of high fever, he did not suffer, and he was mercifully spared from knowing that he was about to quit objects so beloved, and so fondly cherished as his wife and children ever were. His tenderness as a father, who can do justice to?"

In addition to grieving the loss of her father, Austen was now faced with financial worries. In the early nineteenth century, a man's estate, upon his death, went to his nearest male relative—in this case her brother James. Austen, Cassandra, and their mother were dependent upon the generosity of their male relatives to keep them in relative comfort—Frank, James and Henry each offered some support to help, but the women were forced to move to a more modest apartment until they could decide where they would next go.

Almost everyone seemed to feel that Edward would assume the greatest responsibility for the women. Edward, the wealthiest son, with several homes, did not immediately offer one of these to his mother. Instead, an invitation was sent to Cassandra to come and stay with his family at Godmersham—to help care for his children.

It was a terribly bleak time for Austen. Now twenty-nine with almost no resources and dependent upon her brothers' generosity for her very subsistence, it seemed clear that she could offer nothing to a prospective husband. She briefly considered teaching, but rejected it as perhaps the worst fate that could await her.

Throughout 1806, the Austen women lived in transit, guests of James and Mary at Steventon, guests of the Biggs at Manydown (no doubt an awkward visit, considering that Austen had rejected Henry Bigg's proposal), in temporary housing back at Bath, and then as guests of their cousins the Leighs, first in Gloucestershire and then in Warwickshire. Later in the year, they visited Edward Cooper in Staffordshire and then went back to Steventon. They were joined there by Austen's brother Frank and his new bride, Mary, before traveling on to Southampton, not far from where the Austens had once lived. Mary was to stay with the Austen women when Frank once more returned to sea, but for the time being they all shared a house in Southampton. Cassandra—though not Austen or their mother—had been invited to spend Christmas at Godmersham; Edward had a tenth child and Cassandra's help was once again needed.

This living out of suitcases and never being settled clearly created a sense of impermanence and unease for Austen. Her writing had once again been set aside. Her new sister-in-law,

Did you know...

In Jane Austen's day, respectable young women did not live alone if they were not married. They lived either with their family or with someone their relatives had approved to serve as a kind of guardian or "protector." Without marriage, a young woman like Austen was dependent on her family members, living with her parents if they were alive or with other relatives. If there was not enough family income to support her in this way, a young woman would take a job as governess or paid lady's companion and live with her employer.

Mary, was pregnant, and Cassandra returned in time to help Austen and their mother care for her during the last difficult months of her pregnancy and the baby—a girl—when she was born.

The family moved yet again in the fall of 1807. Edward invited his mother and sisters, as well as James and Mary, to visit with him at one of his homes at Chawton. It was an impressive mansion, with walls covered with elaborate tapestries and huge rooms with walk-in fireplaces. The family then returned to Southampton, where various relatives visited and gave Austen an opportunity to spoil whichever of her nieces and nephews were at hand.

In 1808, Austen spent yet another year traveling from one family member to another, first to visit Henry and Eliza in Brompton, and then on to visit Edward and Elizabeth at Godmersham, traveling with James' wife, Mary, and their two younger children. Austen had looked forward to the trip, but she did not get along with Mary, who complained incessantly throughout the trip. Later in the year, having returned to Southampton, Austen was able to entertain the Bigg sisters, and she and Cassandra spent a happy two weeks with their friends.

Then Cassandra was summoned to Godmersham. Elizabeth's eleventh pregnancy was nearly over, and she wanted her sister-in-law's help. A baby boy was born on September 28; only a few days later, Elizabeth suddenly and unexpectedly died. While Cassandra helped the family at Godmersham, two of Edward's sons— Edward and George—who had been away at school arrived in Southampton, where Austen busied herself in caring for the boys.

Austen generously dedicated herself to keeping Edward's sons busy and occupied, helping them cope with their grief while also giving them opportunity to play. Perhaps it was these actions by Cassandra and Austen that suddenly pricked at Edward's conscience, for he finally offered to provide a house for his mother and sisters.

The women were given their choice of two different homes. They could settle near Godmersham in the small village of Wye, or they could choose a smaller cottage in Chawton. After several weeks of debate, the cottage at Chawton seemed the best option, and Henry traveled there to inspect the home and report back.

Cassandra remained at Godmersham, and on November 21, 1808, Jane wrote to her sister, sharing the information about their future home which Henry had provided, including details of six bedrooms and "garrets for store places." It would be a home in the country, much quieter than the homes they had known recently, but Jane was encouraged by the many friends who claimed to know the place and thought it very pretty, and relieved that, with her brother as their landlord, they would no longer need to worry about being able to afford the cost of increasing rent or maintenance.

One final matter remained—the fate of *Susan*, the novel that had been sold to the publisher Richard Crosby six years earlier. In April, Austen wrote to the publisher, asking about the novel and offering to supply a second copy if the original had been lost. She received a quick and discouraging response:

MADAM,—We have to acknowledge the receipt of your letter of the 5th inst It is true that at the time mentioned we purchased of Mr. Seymour a MS. Novel entitled Susan, and paid him for it the sum of £10, for which we have his stamped receipt, as a full consideration, but there was not any time stipulated for its publication, neither are we bound to publish it. Should you or anyone else [publish it] we shall take proceedings to stop the sale. The MS. Shall be yours for the same as we paid for it.

Austen did not have the necessary 20 pounds to buy back the rights to her novel, and the publisher's letter made clear that there were no immediate plans on their part to publish it. She was forced to give up this hope, and it would not be until 1816 that she would be able to buy back the rights to the novel that would become known as *Northanger Abbey*.

Austen and her mother settled into Chawton Cottage in 1809. Austen found her new residence far more enjoyable than No. 4 Sydney Place, and began revising Elinor and Marianne *between 1809 and 1810, eventually submitting it as* Sense and Sensibility.

7

Home at Last

AUSTEN AND HER mother were the first to settle into their new home at Chawton Cottage, arriving in July of 1809. Martha Lloyd, the sister of James' wife Mary and an old family friend, had by now become part of the household, and both she and Cassandra arrived at Chawton a short while later.

Austen was overjoyed at the new surroundings and could not help inserting them into a poem she wrote for Frank to celebrate the birth of his second child, a boy:

My dearest Frank, I wish you joy
Of Mary's safety with a Boy,
Whose birth has given little pain
Compared with that of Mary Jane.—

Our Chawton home, how much we find
Already in it, to our mind;
And how convinced, that when complete
It will all other Houses beat
That ever have been made or mended,
With rooms concise, or rooms distended.

As was learned at the beginning of this book, the move to Chawton would signal a new phase in Austen's life—a return to her writing, a time of happiness, and ultimately, a time when her writing would finally be published. Between 1809 and 1810, Austen reworked her novel *Elinor and Marianne*, revising the manuscript and submitting it for consideration under its new title, *Sense and Sensibility*. She had turned to this novel since the rights to *Susan* were still being held by another publishing company and, many years earlier, *First Impressions* (later *Pride and Prejudice*) had been rejected when submitted by her father. This third time, she found a receptive audience. By late 1810, *Sense and Sensibility* had been accepted by the publisher Thomas Egerton.

Austen traveled to London in April 1811 for a visit with Henry and Eliza, and to check over the proofs of *Sense and Sensibility*. The process was slow—Austen only was given a few pages at a time to check—but she was kept busy with parties and social events arranged by Henry and Eliza. She had hoped to leave London with a copy of the new book, but after several weeks she was forced to return to Chawton and wait.

Sense and Sensibility finally appeared in late October, published in three volumes. Its author was listed as simply "A Lady" or, incorrectly in some advertisements as "By Lady A-." Only a few family members and close friends were let in on the secret at the beginning. The initial reviews, which followed a few months later, were all favorable, and encouraged Austen to revise and prepare the novel *First Impressions* for publication. She made some minor alterations, but overall felt that the novel required few changes—with one exception. In the 15 years since she had first written the novel, another book had been published under the same title. Austen began searching for a new title, and found it in one of her favorite novels—*Cecilia* by Miss Burney—where, in the novel's fifth volume, the phrase "Pride and Prejudice" was printed in capital letters and repeated several times. Austen liked the phrase and the symmetry it created with her novel *Sense and Sensibility*. She retitled the novel and submitted it to the publisher Egerton, who paid 110 pounds for the rights to publish it.

In early 1813, as the time neared for *Pride and Prejudice* to appear, Cassandra left for a long-planned visit to James at Steventon. It must have been a bit disappointing to Austen that her family so steadfastly maintained its same routines and schedules without openly acknowledging and celebrating her new success.

She wrote to Cassandra on January 29, 1813, when the book arrived:

> . . . I want to tell you that I have got my own darling child from London. . . . Miss Benn dined with us on the very day of the book's coming, and in the evening we set fairly at it, and read half the first vol. To her, prefacing that, having intelligence from Henry that such a work would soon appear, we had

desired him to send it whenever it came out, and I believe it passed with her unsuspected. She was amused, poor soul! That she could not help, you know, with two such people to lead the way, but she really does seem to admire Elizabeth. I must confess that I think her as delightful a creature as ever appeared in print, and how I shall be able to tolerate those who do not like her at least I do not know.

It is clear from this letter that Austen and her family were still trying to preserve her anonymity. There were also some hurt feelings. At the beginning, Austen did not have enough copies of the new novel to send to all of her brothers and was forced to apologize to Frank and James for not being able to immediately supply them with the volumes of *Pride and Prejudice*.

The reviews of *Pride and Prejudice*, when they appeared, were as favorable as those of *Sense and Sensibility*. The *British Critic* offered this comment: "the story is well told, the characters remarkably well drawn and supported, and written with great spirit as well as vigour." The *Critical Review* also approved Austen's work: "[it] rises very superior to any novel we have lately met with in the delineation of domestic scenes. Nor is there one character which appears flat, or obtrudes itself upon the notice of the reader with troublesome impertinence."

Gradually, more and more friends and family members were let in on the secret of Austen's achievement. Austen had soon turned her attention to another of her novels. In the letter she wrote to Cassandra in January, announcing that copies of *Pride and Prejudice* had arrived, she noted that she was planning to attempt a new novel with a completely different focus: a clergyman's ordination. Although the letter makes it seems as if she were beginning to think about a new book, *Mansfield Park* was actually well under way by the time this letter was written at the end of January 1813.

Mansfield Park was markedly different from Austen's earlier writing. The character of Fanny Price is quite different from Elizabeth Bennet or Elinor Dashwood—quite different, in fact, from Austen herself. Fanny Price is quiet, submissive, and humble. Raised by wealthy relatives, she is seldom noticed—and then only when she is needed to offer assistance. It is the character Mary Crawford who offers witty comments, teases, and pokes fun at the stuffy society around her. This time the witty woman is the one who is most at fault—she will not enjoy a happy ending with the man who she captivates.

On April 25, 1813, Henry's wife Eliza died following a

Did you know...

Although Jane Austen wrote her novels some two centuries ago, they have remained popular, finding new audiences in film or television adaptations. *Pride and Prejudice* has been adapted for film, for a television movie, and for several television miniseries. In 1995, the film version of *Sense and Sensibility* starred Emma Thompson and Kate Winslet, adding to the adaptations previously made for television. Gwyneth Paltrow starred in one movie version of *Emma*, while two other versions were made for TV. *Mansfield Park* was released as a film in 1999, and *Persuasion* and *Northanger Abbey* have both been adapted for television.

long illness at the age of fifty-one. Henry soon came to Chawton and then returned to London with Austen. It was not a sad visit—Eliza had been in pain and discomfort in the final days of her illness and her death had put an end to her suffering. Austen enjoyed the quiet of Henry's home, where she wrote in solitude in the front drawing room and spent time shopping (finally enjoying the advantage of extra money from her writing) and visiting art exhibits.

Austen returned to London again in the fall, this time with Edward and three of her nieces. With Henry's mourning period ended, the family enjoyed visits to the theater, to Covent Garden, and more shopping. Henry made no secret of his sister's role as the author of *Pride and Prejudice* and *Sense and Sensibility*, whose second printing appeared in 1813, and even made a grand production of opening a bank account for her to deposit her earnings.

Back at home, Austen divided her time between her writing and spending time with her nieces and nephews. Fanny, Charles' daughter, was a particular favorite, and she joined the family when Austen read aloud from her novel-in-progress, *Mansfield Park*.

The new book brought less laughter than some of the earlier books had. It was a much more moral work, and Fanny Price was a much more serious character. The book was very black and white in tone; the characters who begin with faults have not overcome them by the novel's end. The novel offers little hope of redemption for those whose bad choices mark them from the start as destined for an unhappy ending.

The novel was finally finished during a visit to Godmersham in the fall of 1813. Austen worked in the elegant library, writing as she sat by the fire. This time, knowing that Henry had not been able to keep the secret of her earlier books, Austen decided that there was little point in trying to hide behind an anonymous name:

> I was previously aware of what I should be laying myself open to; but the truth is that the secret has spread so far as to be scarcely the shadow of a secret now, and that, I believe, whenever the third appears, I shall not even attempt to tell lies about it. I shall rather try to make all the money than all the mystery I can of it. People shall pay for their knowledge if I can make them.

In November 1813, she traveled to London to visit with a sick Henry and present her publisher with the completed manuscript of *Mansfield Park*. Egerton felt the novel was moral and serious—a mixed compliment, as it reflected an attitude that did not necessarily make for best-selling novels. This time, Egerton offered only to buy the novel on commission—the same deal offered for Austen's first novel. They would publish the book, but Austen would need to guarantee that she would cover all the expenses if the book failed to earn back the cost of publication.

By the time she turned thirty-eight, she had already begun to think about a new novel—a novel of humorous and often unintentional mistakes. *Emma* was a dramatic shift from *Mansfield Park*, focusing on a heroine who constantly confuses not only the attitudes and affections of those around her, but even seems to often be unable to clearly understand herself. Austen described her character at the novel's beginning with the memorable phrase: "The real evils, indeed, of Emma's situation were the power of having rather too much her own way, and a disposition to think a little too well of herself." Emma is guided by instinct, but her instinct is constantly and comically proven wrong.

Emma was the fastest of Austen's novels to be completed—she had finished work on it by the end of March 1815—and most critics feel it is her most polished and successful work. As Austen worked away, *Mansfield Park* was published on May 9, 1914. The family was focused more on a challenge to Edward's right to inherit the Knight lands—a lawsuit which, if Edward lost, would force him to give up much of his land, including the Chawton Cottage. Little attention was paid to the newest of Austen's works to be published, and there were few critical reviews of the work.

Mansfield Park did sell out its first printing, and Austen returned to London to meet with Egerton and see if a second edition might be printed. Egerton, however, felt that the novel had not sold as well as Austen's previous books had done and decided against reprinting it. She was disappointed; *Emma* was nearly completed, and when she left London it was with the decision that her next novel would be published by someone else.

When *Emma* was ready for publication, by the summer of 1815, Austen was once more in London. She and Henry decided that the publisher of Lord Byron's poetry might be a suitable choice, and so they visited the successful publisher John Murray, who agreed to read the manuscript. Austen waited impatiently for several weeks until an offer finally came through for 450 pounds for *Emma*, as well as the copyrights of *Mansfield Park* and *Sense and Sensibility.* Henry, who had become quite sick during Austen's visit, was insulted by the offer and, after recovering slightly, attempted to dictate a response, but once again collapsed and seemed so ill that Austen quickly summoned her brothers and sister to London, fearing the worst. Henry finally recovered, and the brothers left him to Cassandra and Austen's care.

Austen, after a meeting with the publisher, finally came to more favorable terms for the publication of *Emma*—2000 copies would be published at her expense; she would pay

Gwyneth Paltrow starred in the title role in the 1996 film adaptation of Emma. *Austen finished the book in 1815 and it is considered by many to be her most accomplished work. In fact, an anonymous review at the time that praised* Emma *and Austen's writing style turned out to have been written by Sir Walter Scott.*

Murray a ten percent commission for the book and retain any additional profits for herself. Murray also agreed that the book would be published within one month—the time by which Austen wanted to leave London.

Austen was taking care of her own business while helping to care for Henry, and the two matters quickly collided. Henry's doctor, a Dr. Baillie, also served as one of the Prince Regent's doctors. He soon informed Austen that the prince (the future King George IV) was an admirer of her novels, and an invitation followed for Austen to visit the prince's palace at Carlton House. The prince himself was not there for this private tour, which probably made it even more enjoyable for Austen. The prince had made a reputation for himself with his frequently scandalous behavior. Still, shocking behavior by the owner was not enough to deter her from the opportunity to have a private tour of a palace. She inspected the elaborate carpets, tapestries, antiques, and the impressive Gothic library with great enjoyment, until her tour guide, Carlton House's librarian, mentioned that the prince had authorized him to say "that if Miss Austen had any other novel forthcoming, she was quite at liberty to dedicate it to the Prince."

Austen was shocked by the suggestion, and though gracious to the librarian, she returned home determined not to do any such thing. Her brother and sister quickly convinced her that the prince would be insulted if she did not do what he so clearly wanted her to do. Austen finally realized that the dedication to the prince might offer some marketing poten- tial for her novel, as well as provide some incentive to her publisher to keep good his promise for a speedy publication.

The novel, with the dedication in place, was published in December 1815. Her family was quick with praise for the new book, and favorable (though not enthusiastic) literary reviews soon followed. The most significant was published in the *Quarterly Review*—an extensive article focusing on Austen's writing whose anonymous author was later revealed to be Sir Walter Scott. Some ten years later, it was clear that Scott's admiration for the Jane Austen style had continued. In his diary, he wrote: "That young lady has a talent for describ- ing the involvements and feelings and characters of ordinary life, which is to me the most wonderful I ever met with."

The publication of *Emma* marked yet another accomplish- ment for Austen. Still more enjoyment followed when she and Henry were able to successfully purchase back the rights to *Susan* (later *Northanger Abbey*), which had remained with the publisher Crosby, unpublished, for thirteen years. After the rights had been regained, they were able—with some pleasure—to inform Crosby that the novel he had never bothered to publish was by the author of *Pride and Prejudice, Sense and Sensibility, Mansfield Park,* and *Emma.*

Emma sold briskly, but it would be the last of her novels published in Austen's lifetime. While she was caring for Henry in London, she had become sick herself. She returned to Chawton to recover and rest.

In March of 1816, Henry was forced to declare bankruptcy. Several banks had failed in the period following the end of the Napoleonic wars, and Henry's was one of them. Henry quickly rebounded, deciding to return to his youthful dream of becoming a clergyman. He eventually followed through on this scheme, becoming the curate of Bentley.

Despite the stress of Henry's financial collapse and her own worries about her health, Austen was already at work on another novel, to be titled *Persuasion.* She had resisted the rather insistent suggestions of the prince's librarian, who at first proposed that she base her next novel on a character who sounded suspiciously like him, and still later that she write a historical romance focusing on the royal House of Saxe Cobourg. Austen politely responded:

> You are very, very kind in your hints as to the sort of composition which might recommend me at present, and I am fully sensible that an historical romance, founded on the House of Saxe Cobourg, might be much more to the purpose of profit or popu-larity than such pictures of domestic life in country villages as I deal in. But I could no more write a romance than an epic poem. I could not sit seriously down to write a serious romance under

any other motive than to save my life; and if it were indispensable for me to keep it up and never relax into laughing at myself or at other people, I am sure I should be hung before I had finished the first chapter. No, I must keep to my own style and go on in my own way, and though I may never succeed again in that, I am convinced that I should totally fail in any other.

The novel *Persuasion*, like Austen's earlier novels, is set in the country, and it is humorous and full of witty observations of society. However, it treats its theme—what role prudence should play in love—with a subtle difference from the way it might have been treated by a younger Austen. In *Persuasion*, there are shades of gray introduced into a theme that before might have been simply depicted in black and white, right or wrong. The heroine, Anne Elliott, gradually realizes that she has failed to properly assess the character of the naval officer she loves. The moral seems to show that emotion and feeling can play as much a role in love (though not the primary role) as simple good sense.

Austen finished her first draft of the novel in July 1816 and then spent a few weeks revising portions that she found flat and unsuccessful. She was not completely satisfied but set it aside and began work on the recovered *Susan*, which was briefly retitled *Catherine* before taking on its final title, *Northanger Abbey*.

Austen was also busy reviewing and commenting on the writing attempts of her nieces and nephews, many of whom had decided that they, too, wanted to become authors like their aunt. By September of 1816, it is clear that her health was affecting her—she wrote to Cassandra (who was in Gloucestershire) on September 8, saying "Thank you, my back has given me scarcely any pain for many days."

Family visits continued into the new year. Although Austen

frequently felt sick, she had begun work on yet another new novel. It would not be completed, but would be published, unfinished, many years later under the title *Sanditon*. The portion that Austen completed is reminiscent of her earlier writing—poking fun at society, particularly at its most melodramatic, silly, and snobby members. Interestingly, considering her own illness, she also targets those people who spend too much time worrying about their health.

At the age of 41, Austen felt her own health declining. The tone of comedy is strong; she may have deliberately chosen the type of story that came easiest to her, as well as one that would make her smile and keep up her spirits. In March 1817, even that would prove too much for her; she put aside the manuscript and did not pick it up again.

She had been finding it increasingly difficult to maintain the habits that had once given her pleasure. In January, too weak to walk, she had for a time used a carriage pulled by a donkey, but soon this was too tiring for her. She spent her days in a bed or stretched out on a kind of makeshift sofa of two or three chairs pushed together. She felt that the real sofa should be reserved for the use of her mother, who had been complaining about her health for many more years.

Austen continued to try to make light of her illness whenever possible, but she must have sensed that the end was near. By the end of March she had prepared a will, leaving everything to her sister Cassandra, apart from a sum for Henry and another to a family friend.

Her niece, Caroline Austen, visited Chawton in early April. She found her aunt's condition greatly deteriorated:

> She was very pale, her voice was weak and low, and there was about her a general appearance of debility and suffering; but I have been told that she never had much acute pain. She was

not equal to the exertion of talking to us, and our visit to the sick room was a very short one, Aunt Cassandra soon taking us away. I do not suppose we stayed a quarter of an hour; and I never saw Aunt Jane again.

By mid-May, Austen was suffering from new symptoms, and her doctor referred her to a specialist in Winchester, about 14 miles away. She and Cassandra, accompanied by Henry, made the trip on May 24, staying at a rented apartment close enough to Winchester Cathedral that they could hear the chimes. Austen's family had rallied around her in her illness, visiting her frequently at Chawton and sending her letters to keep her entertained. Austen's last letter, written three days after her arrival at Winchester, was to her nephew, Edward Austen. She wrote thanking him for his concern about her and reassuring him that she was feeling stronger and better. She offered a brief description of their house, and her enjoyment of being able to use Edward's father's carriage to make the trip. Only at the end does her cheerful facade slip:

> God bless you, my dear Edward. If ever you are ill, may you be as tenderly nursed as I have been, may the same blessed alleviations of anxious sympathising friends be yours, and may you possess—as I dare say you will—the greatest blessing of all, in the consciousness of not being unworthy of their Love. I could not feel this.

It quickly became clear that Austen was not getting better. She would live for only six weeks more, growing weaker though suffering little pain. She continued, almost up to the end, to attempt to remain cheerful and amuse the family members who arrived to keep her company. James and Henry, the clergymen, read religious devotions to her, as she turned increasingly to spiritual reading for comfort in her final days.

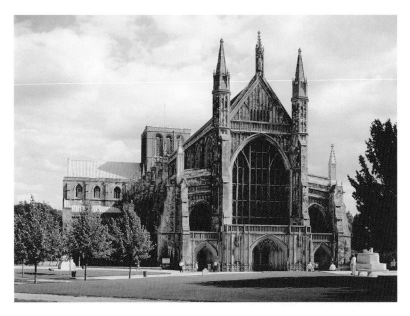

At age 41, Austen started to feel ill while working on her novel Sanditon. Eventually she saw a specialist in Winchester, but it was to no avail. Austen died in 1817 and was buried in the north aisle of Winchester Cathedral.

By the third week of July, the doctor informed James and Henry, who then told Austen, that she would not live much longer. She was able to say her goodbyes to the family members who were with her, before finally growing weaker. She drifted in and out of consciousness, and died early on the morning of July 18, 1817. She was buried in the north aisle of Winchester Cathedral, where a plaque contains the following words:

The benevolence of her heart,
the sweetness of her temper, and
the extraordinary endowments of her mind
obtained the regard of all who knew her, and
the warmest love of her intimate connections.

1775   Jane Austen is born in Steventon, England on December 16.

1785–1786   Attends Abbey School in Reading, England.

1795   *Elinor and Marianne* is probably begun.

1796   Begins writing *First Impressions*.

1797   *First Impressions* is completed, offered to a publisher and rejected. *Elinor and Marianne* is revised and becomes *Sense and Sensibility*.

1798   *Susan* (later retitled *Northanger Abbey*) is probably begun.

1799   *Susan* is completed.

1801   Austen family leaves Steventon and moves to Bath.

1802   Harris Bigg proposes to Austen; she initially accepts but then refuses him.

1803   Austen sells *Susan* to a publisher, but it is never printed.

1805   Austen's father dies.

1807   Austen, her mother, and sister move to Castle Square, Southampton.

1809   Austen, her mother, and sister move to Chawton Cottage.

1810   *Sense and Sensibility* is sold to a publisher.

1811   *Sense and Sensibility* is published; Austen begins work on *Mansfield Park*; begins revisions of *First Impressions* and re-titles it *Pride and Prejudice*.

1812   *Pride and Prejudice* is sold to a publisher.

1813   *Pride and Prejudice* is published; Austen completes and sells *Mansfield Park*.

1814   *Emma* is begun; *Mansfield Park* is published.

1815   *Emma* is completed; *Persuasion* is begun; *Emma* is published.

1816 Rights to *Susan* are bought back; Austen begins revising novel, ultimately retitling it *Northanger Abbey*; *Persuasion* is completed.

1817 *Sanditon* is begun, but then set aside. Austen dies on July 18.

Sense and Sensibility (1811)

Pride and Prejudice (1813)

Mansfield Park (1814)

Emma (1815)

Northanger Abbey (1817)

Persuasion (1817)

SENSE AND SENSIBILITY

Sense and Sensibility was first published in 1811. It tells the story of two sisters, Elinor and Marianne Dashwood, and their different approaches to life and romance. Elinor is sensible—she is more practical and her behavior is guided by basic principles of self-control and good breeding. Marianne is more sensitive, guided by her emotions and feelings. The novel comically reveals how love can be impacted by society and vice versa.

PRIDE AND PREJUDICE

Pride and Prejudice was first published in 1813. Originally titled *First Impressions*, the plot focuses on the false first impressions Elizabeth Bennett makes of Mr. Darcy, and he of her, and how events force them to gain very different insight into the true character of the other.

EMMA

Emma tells the story of young, wealthy Emma Woodhouse, who occupies herself by matchmaking, with frequently unintentionally comic results. The novel reveals a young woman in a small society who gains a much greater understanding of the world—and herself.

ELIZABETH BENNET—the heroine of *Pride and Prejudice*. She wins the heart of Mr. Darcy by behavior different from that of traditional romantic heroines, by her willingness to behave unconventionally, and by her lively mind.

ELINOR AND MARIANNE DASHWOOD—the two sisters from *Sense and Sensibility*, whose contrasting approaches to life and love demonstrate the difference between behavior guided by emotion and that guided by good sense.

EMMA WOODHOUSE—the heroine of *Emma* is rich and attractive. She is also young and completely confident in her matchmaking skills, despite being constantly and consistently proven wrong. She attempts to pair up those around her, oblivious to their true feelings—and hers.

An Austen Chronology.
www.lang.nagoya-u.ac.jp/~matsuoka/Austen-Chro.html

Austen.com.
www.austen.com

Austen, Jane. *The Complete Novels of Jane Austen*. New York: The
Modern Library, 1988.

Austen-Leigh, William and Richard Arthur Austen-Leigh. *Jane Austen:
Her Life and Letters*. 2nd ed. New York: Russell & Russell, 1965.

Bloom, Harold, ed. *Jane Austen: Modern Critical Views*. New York:
Chelsea House Publishers, 1986.

Cecil, David. *A Portrait of Jane Austen*. New York: Hill and Wang, 1979.

Chawton House Library.
www.chawton.org

Copeland, Edward and Juliet McMaster, eds. *The Cambridge Companion
to Jane Austen*. New York: Cambridge University Press, 1997.

A Guide to the Jane Austen Collection.
www.goucher.edu/library/jausten/jane.htm

Hampshire, Inspirational Home of Jane Austen.
www.hants.gov.uk/austen/

Internet Movie Database entry for Jane Austen.
www.us.imdb.com/M/person-exact?Austen,%20Jane

The Jane Austen Centre in Bath, England.
www.janeausten.co.uk

The Jane Austen Society of North America.
www.jasna.org

Myer, Valerie Grosvenor. *Jane Austen: Obstinate Heart*. New York:
Arcade Publishing, 1997.

Nokes, David. *Jane Austen: A Life*. New York: Farrar, Straus and Giroux, 1997.

Rees, Joan. *Jane Austen: Woman and Writer*. New York: St. Martin's Press, 1976.

The Republic of Pemberley.
www.pemberley.com

Shields, Carol. *Jane Austen*. New York: Viking Penguin, 2001.

Stewart, Maaja A. *Domestic Realities and Imperia. Fictions: Jane
Austen's Novels in Eighteenth-Century Contexts*. Athens, Ga.: The
University of Georgia Press, 1993.

Stokes, Myra. *The Language of Jane Austen: A Study of Some Aspects of
Her Vocabulary*. London: Macmillan, 1991.

Tomalin, Claire. *Jane Austen: A Life*. New York: Alfred A. Knopf, 1998.

Austen, Jane. *The Complete Novels of Jane Austen*. New York: The Modern Library, 1988.

Austen-Leigh, William and Richard Arthur Austen-Leigh. *Jane Austen: Her Life and Letters*. 2nd ed. New York: Russell & Russell, 1965.

Cecil, David. *A Portrait of Jane Austen*. New York: Hill and Wang, 1979.

Myer, Valerie Grosvenor. *Jane Austen: Obstinate Heart*. New York: Arcade Publishing, 1997.

Nokes, David. *Jane Austen: A Life*. New York: Farrar, Straus and Giroux, 1997.

Shields, Carol. *Jane Austen*. New York: Viking Penguin, 2001.

Tomalin, Claire. *Jane Austen: A Life*. New York: Alfred A. Knopf, 1998.

www.astoft.co.uk/austen/
[Jane Austen Places]

www.austen.com
[Austen.com Jane Austen site]

www.chawton.org
[Chawton House Library]

www.hants.gov.uk/austen/
[Hampshire, Inspirational Home of Jane Austen]

www.janeausten.co.uk
[The Jane Austen Centre in Bath, England]

www.janeaustenmuseum.org.uk
[Jane Austen's House on the Web – Austen Museum in Chawton, England]

www.jasna.org
[The Jane Austen Society of North America]

www.pemberley.com
[The Republic of Pemberley – Austen site]

HEATHER LEHR WAGNER is a writer and editor. She earned an M.A. from the College of William and Mary and a B.A. from Duke University. She is the author of more than twenty books for teens, including biographies of great American presidents, famous flyers, and extraordinary women.

UNION PUBLIC LIBRARY
Friberger Park
Union, New Jersey 07083